Praise for Brave New Mind

"For me, *Brave New Mind* came to my awareness at the perfect time. Maisel's concepts of 'serene readiness' and 'prime directives' read like meditative life preservers. At this very difficult moment in human history, a new paradigm of thought is called for, and Maisel has just the intellect to create it for us. I encourage any thinking person to add this book to their mental/literary arsenal immediately!"

—Rahti Gorfien, author of *The Five Emotions that Stop Success in Coaches, Clients, and Creatives*

***

"*Brave New Mind* is an essential and timely work. Dr. Maisel masterfully unpacks the psychological pressures of modern life and offers a compelling path forward through *serene readiness*. His insights challenge conventional thinking and empower readers to reclaim their mental clarity and purpose.

Thoughtful, engaging, and deeply relevant, this book is a must-read for anyone seeking a more intentional, self-directed life. I highly recommend it!"

—Randy Cima, PhD, psychologist and child advocate

***

"Eric Maisel's book, *Brave New Mind*, is a powerfully insightful and highly instructive manual not only for surviving in today's brave new world, but thriving in it. Instead of presenting mere 'coping' mechanisms for dealing with the fast-paced, oppressive nature of modern reality, Maisel shows us in a very practical way how we can hone our minds to be serenely ready for whatever comes at us. Doing so transforms the depression, anxiety, and general unhappiness that our world causes into a strong, joyful, and creative life."

—Adam Zwig, psychologist and touring musician

***

"Thought-provoking and original, Eric Maisel takes the reader on a philosophical journey through 'mind,' with much to reflect on along the way. Recommended."

—Derek Summerfield, psychiatrist, Kings College London and London Institute of Psychiatry

***

"Eric Maisel's latest asks us to look at how we are using our minds in these difficult times and invites us to meet our current challenges with 'serene readiness,' a brand-new paradigm with the power to save lives."

—Risa Williams, author of *Get Stuff Done Without the Stress*

***

"*Brave New Mind* is a timely and insightful reflection on the chaos of modern life and the kind of mental resilience we need to navigate it. Maisel makes a compelling case for why cultivating 'serene readiness' is more important than ever. This book is an invitation to think differently and to approach life with a deeper sense of awareness and purpose."

—The Fio Bros, hosts of the *BestSelf University* podcast

***

"If you read only one book to help you cope and thrive amidst these complex and changing times we are living in, read this one. Make this the book the encouragement you give to yourself and to everyone you love."

—Lynda Monk, MSW, RSW, CPCC, leader of the International Association for Journal Writing [IAJW.org]

***

"With the kind of page turning usually saved for great dramas or thrillers, I just finished reading Eric Maisel's latest book, *Brave New Mind*. Maisel presents a picture of the dire realities we're facing in today's world, along with proposals for how we can not only survive but thrive, in a style that is both gentle and hard-hitting, with just enough humor to make the deep material comprehensible and entertaining. As is the case with many of Eric Maisel's works, *Brave New Mind* is a book I can see reading over and over. It will never grow old or obsolete."

—Denise Beck-Clark, MFA, MSW; author of *Concurrent Sentences: A True Story of Murder, Love, and Redemption*

***

"*Brave New Mind* by Eric Maisel is a thought-provoking exploration of the mental resilience required to navigate the complexities of contemporary life. With a blend of philosophy, psychology, and cultural critique, Maisel presents the concept of "serene readiness"—a state of mind that embraces both acceptance and proactive engagement with life's challenges. Maisel's writing is both incisive and urgent, calling readers to develop a mindset capable of withstanding the pressures of an increasingly fragmented world. *Brave New Mind* is a profoundly introspective and timely work, offering readers practical tools for fostering clarity, resilience, and a renewed sense of agency in their lives."

—Juliana J. Bruno, Transformational Coach, podcaster, and author of *Reasons to Live*

***

"How do you stay sane in the modern world? Maisel has an answer. In an accessible style, he combines his wide reading of philosophy with his experience as a psychotherapist in a truly valuable synthesis. It is not a plot spoiler to say that he advocates what to some people may seem an impossible paradox: that we need to cultivate an inner serenity at the same time as a readiness to act. If we do this, we will be able to maintain our sanity and our integrity."

—Martin Adams, existential psychotherapist, author of *An Existential Approach to Human Development: Philosophical and Therapeutic Perspectives*

***

"If you find yourself overwhelmed by the frenzy of modern life or yearning for a deeper sense of purpose and calm, this book offers both intellectual clarity and emotional sustenance. It doesn't promise to make life easy—rather, it offers something far more valuable: a way to bring meaning and purpose to your life, even in turbulent times. *Brave New Mind* isn't just a book; it's a trusted companion, providing the tools to face reality with courage and to cultivate serenity without escapism."

—Stacy Giguere, PhD, Professor of Psychology

***

"Living in a turbulent world creates turbulent minds, but in Maisel's latest book, he lays out a map for navigating such a world with integrity, ease, and serenity. If you want to rid your life of frustration and chaos and discover joyful days again, this is the book for you. Maisel puts forward ways in which we can respond positively to our new realities and preserve our calm and sanity. A life in support of both serenity and action is the goal, and the plan for this is on offer in *Brave New Mind*."

—Roccie Hill, Amazon and Barnes & Noble bestselling author of *The Blood of My Mother* and author of the forthcoming *The Wounds of My Father*

Brave New Mind

Mastering the Art and Practice of Serene Readiness in Stressful Times

Eric Maisel, PhD

Books That Save Lives

Published by Books That Save Lives, an imprint of Jim Dandy Publishing, LLC

Cover Design: Jodie Anders

Published by BTSL/Jim Dandy Publishing
6252 Peach Avenue
Van Nuys, CA 91411
info@jimdandypublishing.com

For bulk orders, special quantities, course adoptions, and corporate sales, please email info@jimdandypublishing.com

ISBN: (print) 978-1-963667-26-4, (ebook) 978-1-963667-27-1

BISAC: SEL024000; PSY008000; PSY022060

Printed in the United States of America

Contents

For Ann, 48 years into this adventure
And for Ethan, Abby, Ellie, Katya, & Kamila

Other Books by Eric Maisel

NONFICTION [as author]:

Affirmations for Artists

Affirmations for Self-Love (with Lynda Monk)

The Art of the Book Proposal

Artists Speak

The Atheist's Way

Become a Creativity Coach Now!

Brainstorm

Coaching the Artist Within

Choose Your Life Purposes

Creative Recovery

The Creativity Book

Creativity for Life

Deep Writing

Everyday You

Fearless Creating

The Future of Mental Health

Helping Parents of Diagnosed, Distressed, and Different Children

Helping Survivors of Authoritarian Parents, Siblings, and Partners

Humane Helping

Life Purpose Boot Camp

The Life Purpose Diet

Lighting the Way

Living the Writer's Life

Making Your Creative Mark

Mastering Creative Anxiety

Overcoming Your Difficult Family

Parents Who Bully

Performance Anxiety

The Power of Daily Practice

Redesign Your Mind

Rethinking Depression

Secrets of a Creativity Coach

60 Innovative Cognitive Strategies for the Bright, the Sensitive, and the Creative

Sleep Thinking

Ten Zen Seconds

Toxic Criticism

20 Communication Tips at Work

20 Communication Tips for Families

The Van Gogh Blues

Unleashing the Artist Within

What Would Your Character Do?

Why Smart, Creative and Highly Sensitive People Hurt

Why Smart People Hurt

Why Smart Teens Hurt

Write Mind

Writers and Artists on Devotion

Writers and Artists on Love

A Writer's Paris

A Writer's San Francisco

A Writer's Space

NONFICTION [as editor]:

Artists in Crisis (editor, with Arnoldo Cantu, forthcoming 2025/2026)

Critiquing the Psychiatric Model (editor, with Chuck Ruby)

Deconstructing ADHD (editor)

Existential Wellness (editor, with Don Laird and Arnoldo Cantu, forthcoming 2026)

Hearing Critical Voices (editor)

Humane Alternatives to the Psychiatric Model (editor, with Chuck Ruby)

Inside Creativity Coaching (editor)

Institutionalized Madness (editor, with Arnoldo Cantu)

Practical Alternatives to the Psychiatric Model of Mental Illness (editor, with Arnoldo Cantu and Chuck Ruby)

The Coach's Guide to Completing Creative Work (editor, with Lynda Monk)

The Creativity Workbook for Coaches and Creatives (editor)

The Great Book of Journaling (editor, with Lynda Monk)

Theoretical Alternatives to the Psychiatric Model of Mental Disorder Labeling (editor, with Arnoldo Cantu and Chuck Ruby)

Transformational Journaling for Coaches, Therapists, and Clients (editor, with Lynda Monk)

FICTION:

Aster Lynn

The Black Narc

The Blackbirds of Mulhouse

Dismay

The Fretful Dancer

The Pen

The Kingston Papers

Murder in Berlin

Settled

MEDITATION DECKS:

Everyday Calm

Everyday Creative

Everyday Smart

PROGRAMS:

Creativity Coach Certificate Program

Existential Wellness Coach Certificate Program

Relationship Coach Certificate Program

Author's Note

This year I'm celebrating fifty-five years of book writing. If you count the "book" I wrote at the age of eight, that would make seventy years of writing books. And what I notice is that my themes have hardly changed over the decades.

I'm interested, and remain interested, in human nature; in the contours of the creative personality and the creative life; in the terrible ways that authoritarianism manifests; and in the complexities of our multiple life purposes and our efforts to make and sustain meaning.

If you're interested in topics of this sort, you will naturally also be intrigued by the properties of the human mind. I've been fascinated by how the mind thinks as the body sleeps (*The Magic of Sleep Thinking*), by the important differences between productive obsessions and unproductive obsessions (*Brainstorm*), and by the idea that the mind can be conceived of as a "room" that one can redesign and redecorate (*Redesign Your Mind*).

Now that we are facing new challenges and new realities, we require a new look at the mind. That's what this book does. In it, I propose a way of mentally and emotionally surviving these unprecedented times by marrying the ancient idea of serenity with the new idea of "readiness."

A person who achieves this "serene readiness" is both at peace in the world and nimble enough to deal with our turbulent times.

In these pages, you'll discover a new way to experience "now." We have thousands of years of descriptions of one way to experience now, the way captured by the Zen Buddhist aphorism, "When you peel a potato, just peel a potato." I would like to teach you a different way, one more suited to the pressing needs of a contemporary creative, sensitive, thinking person. I hope that you'll find this "new way" truly valuable.

I look forward to hearing from you and assisting you as you journey to the place of serene readiness that this book describes. Thank you and good luck!

Introduction to Brave New Mind

by Lynda Monk, MSW, RSW, CPCC

I have been attempting to write the introduction to *Brave New Mind* numerous times over the past couple of weeks. Each time I sat down to work on it, some pressing priority and crisis seemed to drop into my midst. They weren't small things, but big things that needed my attention and that caused various stressors and consequences, things like our youngest son sustaining injuries that required emergency medical care.

Life is like that. We are doing what we do, staying focused and diligent with this and that, while so many other things vie for our attention, distract us, and perhaps worry us as well. For instance, right now, as I write this, I am deeply saddened by a tragedy that took place in Vancouver, BC, Canada, in the province where I live. Yesterday, during the Filipino festival of Lapu Lapu, there was a deadly car-ramming attack by a lone driver, an attack that as of a few minutes ago has reportedly left eleven people dead and many others seriously injured.

I don't share this to depress us, but rather to emphasize what we all know to be true: Life is difficult and stressful, and everywhere we turn there are new things that affect us and evoke our concern. This includes political upheavals, climate destabilization, wars, economic doom, human rights violations, increased homelessness, fatal drug overdoses, the rise in mental health crises, authoritarian regimes, and all the acute and chronic stressors of modern life at this particular time in human history. It is clear we are living with conditions that threaten to break us as human beings. As Eric Maisel asserts, these conditions are *already* breaking us in a variety of ways, individually and collectively.

Brave New Mind invites us to open to a new way of being and thinking; it invites us to ask ourselves new questions and to get curious about what is possible. What does it mean to thrive and flourish and find our way to the qualities and states of mind that we need in order to live happy, healthy, and meaningful lives in the midst of chaotic and changing times?

Eric Maisel's *Brave New Mind: The Art and Practice of Serene Readiness* offers a heartful and prescriptive answer to this most important question. This book is filled with stories, teachings, and calls to action that meet us right where we are as we struggle with the complexity of our times. While reading this book, I found myself nodding, laughing, crying, breathing deeply, and tuning into my own state of *serene readiness*, a concept Maisel offers us that feels like a hopeful and timely invitation.

Maisel is a master poet of chapter and book titles. Each word in the title of this book and its key concepts is worth looking at more closely. What do these words really mean to me, and what do they mean to you?

To me, "brave" means showing courage in the face of uncertainty and dealing with difficult situations without giving up.

"New" is something recently created, unfamiliar, and different from what has previously been known. "New" is filled with possibility.

Our "mind" is that part of us that thinks, feels, remembers, focuses, and makes sense of our experiences.

"Serene" means calm and peaceful. "Serene" just feels good. It is like a place of retreat and refuge within.

"Readiness" means being prepared, even if we're not sure for what.

There is a whole world in each one of these words, and in this book too, a world that offers support, hope, and practical tools for nourishing serene readiness in our minds and lives.

Maisel writes, "This might well do as our essential definition of serenity: Peaceful thoughts abound." But how do we achieve a state where "peaceful thoughts abound?" How do we cultivate our brave new mind amidst the crisis and chaos and stress that seem to be the norm in daily life these days?

Eric Maisel tells a story of his grandfather's stool from when he worked in the garment industry many years ago. That stool had four sturdy legs; hence Maisel's four pillars for fostering our brave new mind, which include needing and having the following: a pertinent philosophy of life, a wise psychology of life, artful self-relationship, and a tool kit for self-support.

A *"brave new mind"* skillfully and compassionately offers this pertinent philosophy and a robust tool kit. This is an important book, one that helps us discover and activate our brave new minds. It will help you stay steady, not break, and be serenely ready for what this life asks of you—what it is asks of all of us, now and next.

With the help of Maisel's teachings and encouragement, serene readiness awaits you. It's like a quiet dawn, when the world holds still with morning light on the waiting sea. You pause looking at the water, stretch your arms up over your head, steady your heart, and nakedly cold plunge into your brave new mind. Come along. Trust yourself and dive in!

Chapter 1

Exchanging Minds

Why a brave new mind is absolutely
crucial

We've all been rushing about with no chance of catching up.
We desperately need a brave new mind that can take into
account our brave new world, a world at once strange and
inhuman, awash with material goods and loneliness,
orchestrated by feckless billionaires more powerful than
governments, where our conversations are with AI chat boxes
and our thinking is reduced to refining the questions that we
ask AI.

What sort of world is this? In the old days, a mere fifty years
ago, you might have chosen to either dodge the rat race or
give in to the rat race, but at least the race was explicable. You
wore a suit and toed the company line, maybe while keeping
half an eye on the lookout for a better job. Now you are a
ping-pong ball bouncing about in a global game, all wrapped
up in side hustles, start-ups, and hundred-hour weeks, while
glued to a device, your phone, that is the slave master of this
brave new world.

Few people are happy nowadays. Were people ever happy? On any hot, humid summer night in Brooklyn, back in the 50's, everyone would be out, because it was too hot to sleep: the grownups sitting on folding chairs at midnight, gossiping, the children listening to music on the radio or playing night games in the cellars and on the roofs of tenements. Happy? Maybe not. But it made sense. It was settled. It was possible to laugh, or at least smile. And now?

We have moved from the center not holding to *nothing* holding. Rightly or wrongly, we trusted doctors. Now, how can you trust a doctor who is willing to prescribe medication aimed at helping you grow longer eyelashes? We trusted the reality and physicality of a five-dollar bill. Now it's swipes and crypto. We trusted that an exotic locale would feel exotic. Now, it's plastic trinkets from China in some far-flung Borneo market. What can possibly be trusted?

At some point, the center stopped holding. Now, the future has stopped holding. We are without a future, and we know it. Without stretching our imagination in the slightest, we can picture the oceans filled with garbage and mega-yachts, gargantuan yachts floating in seas of garbage. We know we are heading there. And there, among the garbage, are lanky pirates in canoes paddling like mad toward some vulnerable mega-yacht. There is the future.

Many minds will simply crash. Millions upon millions of minds will not be able to sustain coherence, motivation, hope, or anything. They will descend into pits with names like depression, anxiety, addiction, suicide. We see this happening everywhere and every day. These happenings are called "epidemics," to make us think that they are passing contagions and not markers of catastrophe. No need to worry, folks, we are still on track for "mental health." Just give the pill companies more leeway. And what jolly ads they run!

The individual puts all of this on his or her own shoulders. My coaching clients are not angrily denouncing the world as it is. They are bemoaning their own shortcomings. They are down on themselves, not the world, because that looks to be the logical default place to point. The world is not making me not write my novel, they think. I myself am not writing my novel. Isn't that obvious?

Is that so obvious? Would we expect Sisyphus to be able to write his novel while rolling his rock up that hill? Would we expect a man who wakes up as a cockroach to just trundle off to his studio and work on his next painting? Would we expect someone with the sure knowledge that Big Brother is watching her to leap out of bed and smile a beaming, innocent smile? Why would we expect that?

We need a brave new mind. It is easy enough to conceptualize —easier at any rate than to achieve—but in this moment, it is indispensable. Without this brave new mind, we find ourselves completely unequal to the times we're living through. This new mind must be able to handle these dystopian realities. Our old mind maybe had to compartmentalize a famine in Ethiopia or an earthquake in China away from everyday awareness and get on with its day. The walls of those nice, neat compartments are all gone now. Now we stand naked in the spotlight. Our old mind can't stand that. Our new mind must. Ready or not, it is time for a transplant.

Chapter 2

Serene Readiness

What this new mind must be able to do

This brave new mind must be able to do two things at once. It must serenely surrender to a dystopian, even unbearable reality. At the same time, it must stand ready at every moment to fulfill its self-created prime directives. That is, it must achieve *serene readiness* in the context of honoring and living its life purposes.

We can analogize to a racer in her stance just before a hundred-meter dash. That racer is not in her stance to experience "the power of now." She has organized her complete being into potential readiness, to be actualized the split second the gun goes off. She is in that stance *for a purpose*.

However, she is not in that stance because that is her *only purpose* in life. Rather, she is in that stance in anticipation of doing the next right thing in her life, which is to run fast. If she were about to have a conversation with her mother about her mother's drinking, she would not find herself in a three-point stance. Rather, she might find herself pacing up and down a hospital corridor or preparing herself as she drove across town to confront her mother.

Her purpose would be different and her actions would be different, but if she had achieved this brave new mind, she would be experiencing the same serene readiness as when she awaited the starter's gun. She is not pacing for the sake of pacing or driving for the sake of driving. She is preparing herself and making herself ready, and she is calm, even if she is also pacing, or even if her hands are tightly gripping the steering wheel.

Let's say that there is neither a race to run nor a confrontation to endure but nothing in particular coming next. It is just a so to speak ordinary moment in a so to speak ordinary day. Ah, but is any such thing really permitted any longer? Isn't every moment now pregnant with need? It may not be pregnant with a precise need—there may be no race to run two minutes from now—but it is nevertheless pregnant with our general need to attend to our life purposes.

Leisurely days secure in their lack of purpose are long gone. A young Alice can drift off into innocent sleep and conjure white rabbits, but we do not have that luxury. A crucial feature of our current reality is that every day is a juggling act where we try to maintain some contact with our many life purposes. If we are not able to maintain that contact and live those purposes, we stand in abject defeat. We have disappointed ourselves, and we know it.

If we don't press ourselves about keeping up the health regimen that will keep our chronic illness from worsening, who will? Mustn't we monitor whether or not we are working on our novel, or if our financial advisor is advising us wisely, or whether or not our alcohol intake has crossed over from social to alcoholic drinking? As a result of this necessary monitoring, we find ourselves confronted by actions to take, and then we must take them. If, for example, we know that we should move three thousand miles away from our bullying father, yet we still haven't made that move, well, then, our situation hasn't changed, has it?

We can't surrender to doing nothing or doing not much, since then we will have failed ourselves, and that failure is what bites and what matters. What we must surrender to is this idea of a new serenity, on the one hand, and a new and genuine readiness, on the other.

Personally, I am writing this with my full attention. But I must also stand ready to hear bad news about the world, stand ready to not react when I notice yet another indignity (unless taking action is the next right thing for me to do), and stand ready to stop everything if our neighbor, who has become a violent drunk, starts pounding on our door.

Our brave new mind supports this new way of being. To achieve it, we are obliged to engage in a certain sort of surrender, one that not only doesn't preclude taking action but that powerfully supports the actions we are obliged to take. This is not white-flag surrender but a version of what Dante asserted that we must do at the gates of Hell: give up our hope of salvation. Nothing will save us—and still we have our work to do.

Chapter 3
Dante Today
Surrendering to complexity

This serenely ready mind has conjoined two ideas. First, it accepts the sentiment captured in Dante's famous line about what to do upon entering Hell: Abandon all hope. We now have completely stopped hoping for utopia, a different world, a different outcome, more ease, or salvation in a second home by the lake. It is not that this is hell on earth: It simply is what it is. We do not hope for an immortality pill or that we will find a better life on Mars. No more of that fantasizing or wishful thinking. We live here, in this reality, facing the facts of existence.

This is why you are working to become serenely ready, for the complications, which are the hallmark of our times. We are completely awash with complexity. Apart from the simplicity of death, what simplicity is now available to us? The simplicity of aging, of becoming feeble and decrepit and not knowing our children from strangers? The simplicity of investing in a company that makes nice returns while ruining rivers? The simplicity of weighing our mate's one-night stand against five thousand nights of loyalty? Not a thing is simple!

Maybe life was never simple. But now complexity is thrust in our faces. You can't fail to appreciate the reality of the current high tides of complexity except through massive denial or some other ego defense that never worked well and that has now dramatically stopped working. Imagine trying to deny the world's inequitable distribution of wealth. What kind of psychological contortions could blind you to that reality? Who could say with a straight face that the mighty oligarchs are doing a wonderful job of looking out for the world's starving children?

We've been forced to take a large, unwelcome bite from the apple of knowledge. We now know in our bones that to deny complexity is to live wrapped in a cocoon that can no longer keep out the cold. So, we must surrender to that truth and stand ready to be struck again by that truth. That is a remarkable feature of the serene readiness I'm describing, that it allows you to face this complexity without blinking or faltering.

You are having an ordinary day, drinking tea and working on a sonnet, and suddenly a massive thought stream drowns you wondering why on earth you are writing poetry. With your brave new mind instantly responding to this tear in the fabric of your life, you return to your sonnet. You were ready for this! Indeed, how could you not have been ready for this? In what multiverse would it be possible not to doubt the plausibility of writing poetry? And yet people are flummoxed when this happens!

If you are not ready for this painful thought, you might not only stop work on your sonnet but drift into catastrophe. How far is stopping work on your sonnet from despair? Just across the street, separated only by slippery asphalt, is one thought, that a sonnet is pointless; this leads to a second thought, that everything you've ever attempted and ever might attempt is pointless, and then to a third thought—pick one—that it is time for a bottomless glass of Scotch, or marathon viewing of a sitcom series, or some chemical peace.

Our brave new mind does not welcome complexity. There is nothing welcome about it. Simplicity would be bliss. But like the petitioners at the gates of Hell who heeded Dante's warning, we surrender to the truth that complexity is with us. We stand ready for it. We may not be able to untangle it, but we are not unraveled by it.

Chapter 4
To the Lighthouse
Why off-grid escape will not work

Our brave new mind, if and when we acquire it, is serenely ready to tackle whatever comes its way. It can handle the thoughts that arise to pester it, the demands made on it by its own prime directives, the events dropped into its lap by circumstances, and the plans society has for it: to sell it merchandise, quell it, boss it, auction it off, and own it.

What our brave new mind is not able to do is escape. Of course, it can't escape its body. But it also can't escape the world. It might seem that each of us has two choices, to live embedded in the world or to escape the world. That second, shall we call it romantic option, conjures images of the antihero, the outsider, the beachcomber, the survivalist, the mountain man.

That is what John the Savage attempts to do when he flees to a lighthouse in Aldous Huxley's *Brave New World*. That does not work for him, and eventually he commits suicide. The escape of suicide is available to him, of course, as it is known to every existential thinker. It is just not the escape he had hoped for.

The alternative to that escape attempt is, of course, to not bother trying to escape. We have arrived at the full knowledge that there is no escape, that retreat is inglorious, and that hiding is out of the question. That is where each of us will land. Even if we try to shut out the news, even if we try to shut out people, even if we try to shut out our neighbors and all entertainments, we will still circle back to realizing that such a life is a defeat and not a victory. That isn't how we wanted to live...or can live.

Escape really isn't possible. Even skilled survivalists on the reality show *Alone*, dropped into some wilderness with a handful of assets like an axe, some fish hooks, and a tarp, tend to start starving within days and cracking within weeks. The hardiest among them last an average of seventy-five days, and some call for rescue after just a matter of hours. And these are folks who claim to love being alone! It turns out that they were rather unready to experience such terrible isolation.

If you take yourself to a lighthouse, a Siberian wilderness, an off-grid cabin in Idaho, or a treehouse in the Amazon jungle, have you won or lost? Have you solved the many problems that modern life has posed? Have you made yourself proud— or have you just made yourself scarce? This is a crucial truth about this moment, that escape has become less possible than ever.

We understand the following paradox: The more text messages we send and receive, the colder life becomes. All that connectivity makes for little to no connection. A text message is not a child on your lap or tea with a friend. So, while escape is impossible, this forced distancing is relentlessly growing. We both can't escape and we can't get warm. This is what our brave new mind is obliged to make sense of.

It can't plot its escape or act as if all is well. Neither position is available. Therefore, its serene readiness must be in the service of making sense of this upsetting reality, that while the ice caps are melting, new glaciers of the heart are appearing daily. Can you feel how difficult it must be to achieve *serenity* in this real-life picture?

It seems absurd to imagine that serenity could possibly be available to a contemporary person. Serenity? At this time, in this place? Well, let us bravely continue, in the full knowledge that escape to a lighthouse is not the answer.

Chapter 5

That One Monkey

Looking for causes in all the wrong places

Each of us is trying to reconcile the following three realities: our meaningless universe, our low-grade species, and our personal experience of incoherence. This is on our mind all of the time, whether we quite know it or not. It affects our motivation, it causes despair, it makes us anxious, and the tensions among these three are only getting worse. That's why a brave new mind is needed.

We have examined every corner of the universe, and we can't make believe that it is purposeful. It simply is what it is, as cold as empty space, as implacable as parallel lines never meeting, as unfunny as a meteor strike. Billions of people still resort to religious, spiritual, and occult answers; but billions of others can't. And even for those who claim that the universe is God-made or otherwise purposeful, do they really feel that in their bones?

So, first, there is the relentlessly meaningless universe. Second is our low-grade species. Just as we have peered into every corner of the universe, we have witnessed every aspect of human nature—the news bombards us with the realities of human failings every second of every day. And we know for certain that, on balance, human beings are not okay.

Do individual people have good moments? Yes. Do folks rally around the right things sometimes? Yes. Can we identify and applaud humanistic values? Yes. But against those points of light, we have dictators with their minions and oligarchs with their billions. We have enmity between groups and grudges passed down from generation to generation. We have hatred and deep divides even within families. We know this.

So, we stand forlorn and wonder, "What am I supposed to do with all this?" Or else we bury that question in a riot of activity, of self-harm, of obsessive worry, and every other manner of untethered thought and behavior. We become incoherent to ourselves. Why am I doing this? Why am I bothering with that? Why am I constantly plagued by this other? How can I operate without any real guidance, in a harsh world, surrounded by a not-okay species?

As a result, people are breaking. This "breaking" goes by different names: depression, addiction, workplace dissatisfaction, physical ailments, suicide, loneliness, and so on. People are not coping with these extreme stresses. Nor can the answer be some sort of pill or therapy. We know that, or should know that. Rather, it must be individual self-knowledge that leads to the creation of personal serene readiness necessary to face all this.

How does our culture currently explain this crisis? The prevailing paradigm is the pseudo-medical one, that there is "more illness than previously." Not more difficulty. Not more complexity. Not more stress. Not more despair. Just more illness. The mental health field has charmingly turned the metaphor of epidemic into common knowledge. Maybe a single monkey, rat, or chicken started all of this mental illness. This is the sad place where we find ourselves, with failed and fraudulent explanations of the pseudo-medical sort.

So, the matter is necessarily returned to you. You know better than to look for that monkey. You know better than to pin a label on yourself and take that to be an explanation. No, honesty is the better path. You accept the realities of human nature, the coldness of space, and all this psychological roiling and say to yourself, "Isn't it truly fascinating that I can chat with myself about these matters? Isn't the right path one of self-conversation?"

Whole societies may collapse, but you can still advocate for your own inner wisdom. Wild winds may whip at your curtains, but those winds need not ruffle your personal coherence. Wouldn't it be better to look for a quiet corner for reflection and not go off and hunt for that non-existent infected monkey, the one being blamed for wreaking all this havoc?

Chapter 6

By the Numbers

A glancing look at the statistics of despair

Do we need numbers to prove the vast scope of this problem? I doubt it. We understand it in our bones without a need for statistics. Nor can we trust the numbers, any more than we can trust the report of blind men encountering an elephant. Each statistic only offers a kind of glancing blow at our subject. But statistics may still be useful in a suggestive way. Here are some:

- In 2023, 700,000 people committed suicide worldwide. In the United States, 1.7 million individuals attempted suicide, 3.5 million people made suicide plans, and 12.3 million contemplated suicide. And who knows what the *real* numbers might be?
- According to the World Health Organization, 280 million people worldwide are currently affected by depression.
- Over 40 million adults in the United States, or fully 20% of America's adult population, are currently suffering from anxiety.

- The current claim is that one in six children aged 5-16 likely has a "mental health problem." This figure has gone up by 50% in the last three years. Between 2021 and 2022 alone, the proportion of British young people aged 17-19 with a probable "mental health disorder" jumped from one in six to one in four.

- 46.8 million Americans aged 12 and older battled a substance use disorder in the past year. That's almost 17% of the population. 10.5% of Americans twelve and older reported an alcohol use disorder in the past year and about 27.2 million Americans twelve or older (9.7% of the population) reported battling a drug use disorder in the past year.

- In the United States, 50% of workers reported feeling stressed at their jobs on a daily basis, 41% reported being worried at work, 22% reported being sad, and 18% reported being angry. Gallup's State of the Global Workplace 2022 report found that workers were experiencing staggering rates of both disengagement and unhappiness. 60% of people reported being emotionally detached at work, and 19% reported feeling miserable.

- The number of fentanyl pills seized by law enforcement increased astonishingly between 2017 and 2023. In 2017, 49,657 pills were seized. In 2023, 115,000,000 pills were seized. That's a 20,000 percent increase!

One-third of Americans report symptoms of either depression or anxiety. All the statistics that measure human difficulty, whether that difficulty is suicidal thinking, depression, anxiety, addiction, or unhappiness at work, are on the rise. These numbers are regularly misinterpreted, but they can't be ignored. These are all markers of psychological collapse and intense stress reactions.

Then there are the sorts of stress reactions where statistics are not kept. In the animal world, there are seven characteristic reactions to stress. Let's quickly run through them.

First are physical symptoms. Animals under stress experience changes in heart rate, respiration rate, blood pressure, appetite, and sleep patterns.

Second are behavioral changes. Animals under stress display increased aggression, increased irritability, increased pacing and hyperactivity, increased withdrawal and avoidance behaviors, and an increase in repetitive behaviors.

Third, in social species, stress can affect an animal's interactions with others. Animals withdraw from social interactions, become more solitary, or exhibit aggressive behavior towards other animals.

Fourth, stress in animals tends to reduce fertility, create changes in mating behaviors, and inhibit reproductive processes.

Fifth, prolonged or severe stress can weaken an animal's immune system, making them more susceptible to illness and disease. Chronic stress contributes to the development of various health problems over time.

Sixth, animals attempt to escape from the source of stress. This might involve trying to flee from a threatening situation or pacing and exhibiting signs of agitation.

Seventh, animals may freeze or become immobile in response to stress. This behavior can serve as a defense mechanism in certain situations, such as when faced with a predator.

We have no statistics on people freezing, or trying to flee, or unable to conceive because hope in the future has faded. We have no statistics on the relationship between despair and immune system disorders or between psychological catastrophe and social withdrawal. We have no statistics on the relationship between meaninglessness and sleep disruption or between dismay at human nature and increased irritability. But we can feel the reality of all that in our bones, can't we?

Taken together, both the places where we have numbers and the places where we don't, a clear picture emerges. People are breaking.

Chapter 7
Metaphors and Analogies

Is it a machine, a beehive, a lantern,
a tidal wave?

The mind is quite something. On the one hand, it can calculate. On the other hand, it operates so to speak psychologically, causing us to hate this person or run off with that person. So, to call it a calculating machine will not do it justice. But to speak only to its psychological machinations will not do it justice, either. And we'd have to bring in memory, and nostalgia, and how it can at times take notice of small things in gigantic spaces and drop a grouse at two hundred yards. The brain/mind can do all that.

Let's take a quick look at some of the bewildering number of metaphors and analogies that have been floated as ways of describing or explaining the mind. Of course, there are all the computer analogies and the ways in which the rise of artificial intelligence is making us rethink what "thinking" and "consciousness" and "mind" might mean. But in addition to all that, we have the following, too.

Clouds in the Sky: Thoughts drift across the mind like clouds, some light and fleeting, others heavy with rain, yet always in motion.

Spider's Web: The mind weaves connections like a spider builds its web, intricate and sticky, catching bits of information and ideas.

Garden of Ideas: The mind is a garden where seeds of thought are planted, some growing wild and chaotic, others cultivated with care.

Echo Chamber: The mind reverberates like an echo chamber, repeating and amplifying certain thoughts while muffling others.

Lantern in the Fog: The mind illuminates just a portion of its vast expanse, revealing what lies ahead but leaving much in shadow.

Beehive: The mind buzzes with activity like a beehive filled with workers (thoughts), each on a mission, sometimes swarming chaotically.

Maze of Mirrors: The mind is a maze of mirrors, reflecting and distorting thoughts, making it hard to distinguish reality from illusion.

Tidal Ocean: Thoughts rise and fall like ocean tides, predictable in cycles yet capable of sudden storms or calm tranquility.

Constellation Map: The mind connects disparate thoughts into patterns, like constellations forming stories out of scattered stars.

Conveyor Belt: The mind operates like a conveyor belt, bringing thoughts forward one after another, some worth keeping and others discarded.

Charming, yes? But none of these capture what it's like to be human, to be embedded in reality, or to think as a human being thinks, with human concerns about good and evil, success and failure, and thirty-year-old grudges.

These metaphors and analogies hardly capture the interior life of human beings. In order to understand how our brave new mind operates, we will need to take a fresh look at the mind and create our own metaphors and analogies, however short of the mark they also may fall.

We know that all of the metaphors and analogies of how the mind works, however charming and suggestive they may be, must turn out to be completely inadequate. Lanterns! Spiders! Bees! Well, our analogies and metaphors will prove inadequate, too. But I hope they seem true to life and to your felt experience.

Indeed, I hope that the phrase "brave new mind" is itself suggestive. I hope it connotes the idea that getting a grip on our own mind is a high-bar goal that requires not only understanding, awareness, and ingenuity, but courage, too. It appears that our goal of serene readiness requires that we become a rebel warrior.

Too often, we are held hostage to whatever our mind wants to conjure up by way of worry, doubt, and self-pestering. Too often, we lose those internal battles, where we commit and then fail to follow through, where we announce an intention without any real belief that we mean it, where we hunger for some result but will not move even an inch in its direction. Isn't a rebel warrior needed to deal with these strange doings?

Let us charge up the next hill!

Chapter 8

Dynamic Succession

Choosing our metaphor for how the
mind works

The metaphors and analogies we use to describe the workings
of the mind, as well as to convey our experience of mind, do
not feel quite on point.

Our mind is not a processing machine or a calculating
machine. We do not experience consciousness as a stream,
nor are we usually following one single train of thought all the
way to its conclusion. Something more like an amalgam of
succession, procession, and collision is going on, something
impossible to capture with any single metaphor or analogy.

On the one hand, something seems to be going on that is like
an orderly procession, something as stately as the coronation
parade of a new king. We are, after all, generally coherent to
ourselves, and we can rather often understand how a single
train of thought got us to a desire for cherry pie or to the
decision to leave our marriage. One thought followed another,
and here we are.

At the same time, we have the sense that thoughts and feelings are colliding, as students might collide in a narrow school hallway between classes. The collisions are not particularly violent, but there is a lot of drama, energy, and unpredictability. The students do manage to get to their classrooms, usually, but maybe not before a lot has gone on in those few minutes of hall crossing—pacts made, secrets shared, assignments copied.

We experience stately procession. We experience wild collision. And we also experience succession, the feeling that one thought or jumble of thoughts is causing the next thought or jumble of thoughts. Feelings are also in the middle of all that, affecting the succession, so that in flow chart terms, a thought pulls us to a feeling, which pulls us along to a thought, and so on.

These are like the activities of the nephews and nieces of the king who, each in their various ways, are trying to ascend to the throne. The main dynamic at place is succession, the notion of something supplanting or replacing what went before it, while also dynamically caused by what went before it.

I would like to suggest that "dynamic succession" may be the best, most useful, truest, and most versatile phrase for us to employ to capture what our mind actually does all day and all night. Thoughts and feelings succeed one another, not randomly, but according to causes that are sometimes clear and sometimes mysterious, sometimes apparent and sometimes hidden.

If we look in on our mind, we sometimes see the nephews plotting to overthrow the king; and sometimes we do not see them, because they are operating behind closed doors. As to why some information is hidden from us and why some is available—as to why we have both conscious awareness and an unconscious that works in its mysterious ways—that is beyond knowing. But surely a lot of it has to do with our instinctual defensiveness.

As much as we want to know and need to know, we also often prefer *not* to know. We do not want to notice that our first two novels haven't been published if we are trying to write our third novel. We do not want to remember that we have been harmed by our parents, if we are trying to get through a Thanksgiving dinner with them. The knowledge of all that is going on in that dynamic succession is somewhere out of conscious awareness, but that material remains in the corridor's dark corners.

So, we will employ the phrase "dynamic succession" to capture a decent rendering of how the mind actually works. Thoughts and feelings succeed one another, elbow one another, replace one another, and collide with one another, not in a random or disorderly way but according to all sorts of forces, pressures, and instructions. There are the effects of new information, the play of memory, the attempts of the hall monitor to maintain order, and so on. A lot is going on with all those billions of neurons!

The headline, then, which we need to flesh out: Our brave new mind, the one that has achieved serene readiness, has an important job. Besides standing ready and operating serenely, our new mind has the job of not only monitoring this dynamic succession but influencing it. This dynamic succession has a way of running off the rails. But our serenely ready brave new mind helps prevent that.

Chapter 9
Monitoring the Succession

On inner acts of observation and influence

As we monitor our dynamic succession of thoughts and feelings, we are not just aware of them or conscious of them. We are also monitoring them, appraising them, and getting ready to intercede if necessary.

We are asking ourselves questions like, "Is this succession heading me in the right direction?" and "Should I intervene and move this succession in some other direction?" These and similar questions amount to our efforts to get a grip on our own mind.

We are interested in knowing if what we are thinking is appropriate to think at this precise moment. For example, is our dynamic succession aimed in the right direction for that upcoming job interview, or is it inclining toward making us feel weak and incompetent? Is what we are thinking ethically suitable, from our own point of view? For instance, is it really okay with us that we are obsessing about our neighbor's wife? Is that really just fine?

Is our dynamic succession a reaction to something that we can change? For instance, would our dynamic succession head in a different, better direction, and would we think better about ourselves, if we made some fundamental life change? Or maybe only a small but significant change is needed? Are we ready to take such actions—serenely ready?

All of this can be appraised and monitored, and ought to be appraised and monitored, if we want to think what we want ourselves to be thinking and if we want to be heading in the direction of our own choosing.

Most people, however, are not in this habit. Even if they are conscious of their dynamic succession of thoughts and feelings—even if they are aware, for instance, that they are coveting their neighbor's wife or badmouthing themselves before a job interview—that consciousness is not the same thing as really noticing with an eye to influencing.

To put it one way, it is the difference between knowing that you are obsessing and having no recourse but to obsess, and knowing that you are obsessing and being able to interrupt that obsessive thinking. That second way, while difficult, is possible; and that ability is a hallmark of the brave new mind that we are describing.

Consider the following. Imagine the job that a prizefight referee is tasked with performing. The referee's jobs are to stay out of the way, but also to intervene as needed.

He watches carefully. If the fighters are fighting, he stays out of the way. In they are in a clinch, he separates them. If one hits the other below the belt, he issues a warning or deducts a point. Most importantly, if one of the fighters can no longer defend himself, he stops the fight. He has the authority to do this major thing, a thing that may cost bettors millions of dollars. He can stop the fight.

He isn't just watching. Rather, he is ready to intervene. Consciousness of our dynamic succession is like that particular kind of watching. We must stand ready to intervene. Mere consciousness of something is not the same as either ratification or rejection of that thing. A consciousness of good and evil is not the same as you opting to do good or deciding not to be bad. To do what is required means both to monitor and to intervene when necessary.

That referee gets to decide. You, in your position as referee of your mind's eternal dynamic succession of thoughts and feelings, get to decide. You get to decide whether to so to speak step back and let the fighters fight or dive in and separate them. You may not be absolutely certain of whether or not to step in, but you are obliged to make your best guess, just as a referee must make his best guess as to whether a fighter can or can't defend himself. That is our job, to make that sort of best guess.

Like that referee, you monitor; and you intercede if necessary. What might come next, without that intercession, is despair, or a thoughtless action, or a wasted day, or some soothing behavior that you instantly regret. With that intercession, what can come next is renewed serenity, renewed readiness, and the sense that you are deeply attending to the business of right living.

Because you interceded, your mind and your being have not been hijacked by that particular succession of thoughts and feelings. That is a victory, and signal proof that you are cultivating a brave new mind.

Chapter 10

Hall Monitor

Painting a picture of brilliant divided attention

Let's switch the image from referee to hall monitor.

Picture a student at a large high school tasked with being a hall monitor between classes, when the narrow school corridor he is assigned to monitor suddenly floods with students moving from one classroom to another.

It is bedlam; and yet it is orderly and predictable enough that he does not have to pay attention to every student or every student interaction. Yes, over there, Billy is shoving Max. But Billy and Max always shove one another without doing any particular damage to each other or to anyone else, so, nothing to worry about there.

Yes, shoving is prohibited. And so, yes, our hall monitor is likely obliged to shout, "Billy, Max, please stop doing that!" But he is saying that in a pro forma and in a largely unconcerned way. He has noticed something, he has done his duty, but he is not on anything like high alert.

But now, a moment later, a big student pointedly shoves a just-out-of-the-closet smaller student with malicious intent. Maybe the big student doesn't mean to knock the small student to the ground, but he certainly means, if not to injure him, at least to frighten him and to make a point.

Now the hall monitor is in a different situation. If he reports the big student, that is a major matter, because administrators will get involved and some version of "all hell breaking loose" will ensue. If he confronts the big student, and maybe demands that he apologize, he is risking his own skin. And if he does nothing, he will have disappointed himself —and not been a good hall monitor. Unfortunately, and so to speak against his will, he must take notice, as doing nothing does not get him off the hook.

If we think of dynamic succession as that crowded hallway full of things happening, and if we think of that hall monitor as your executive function, your existential intelligence, your self-awareness, or some new name that we might coin, we get a good sense of how your brave new mind might work. It would have as one its roles the role of artful hall monitor—in addition to, and simultaneous with, whatever else it might be doing.

Because it will always be doing something else, besides monitoring...

To make this more like how our mind actually works or can work, we would have to posit that our hall monitor is not only monitoring that hall but is also doing his math homework, which requires more than a little of his attention. That is, his attention must be divided if he is to do both things, to monitor the hall and to solve that difficult math problem. How can he do both? Is that really possible?

Yes, it is indeed possible. We do that all the time. We have a good impressionistic sense of how that works, even if we don't have the words to adequately describe that particular state of divided attention. We know that we do not have to "entirely" leave our math problem if we notice Billy and Max shoving one another, as their roughhousing really doesn't matter. But we do have to stop solving our math problem when the big boy shoves and bullies the small boy.

That is how functional "divided attention" works. We have it in us to both pursue a train of thought and also simultaneously monitor our dynamic succession of thoughts and feelings. That is in our repertoire of thinking abilities.

Our parents could train us to do this, our schools could train us to do this, our training programs could train us to do this, but no one does. Everyone makes the too-simple distinction between "paying attention" (the good thing) and "distraction" (the bad thing). Few have anything to say about the subtleties of divided attention, that state where we can stay fully immersed in a train of thought while at the same time making sure that our inner dynamic succession is not trending toward, say, pain and despair.

Please do get this vision in mind, of our hall monitor who can both succeed at solving his math problem and keep tabs on what's going on in that crowded corridor. That hall monitor has something to teach us.

Chapter 11

Succession, Attention, and Stimulation

How inner and outer constantly collide

Three things happen all at once. There is that dynamic succession of thoughts and feelings going on all the time; maybe this takes the form of bits for the novel you're writing, sudden desires and cravings, or a grudge revisited, and so on.

Second, there is the place where you are currently paying attention, like with the math problem we posited our hall monitor working on.

Third, there is the outside world of stimulation and information. That is also always going on—bombarding us, even.

Take the following example. You are watching television: It's your favorite detective show. You are lost in it, not thinking about anything (or so you think). Behind the scenes, however, thoughts and feelings are interacting and creating the dynamic succession I've described.

Maybe you "unconsciously" think of a mistake you made in your life; you have a sinking feeling; you begin to wonder about your abilities; you doubt that you can make a go of the business you've just started; and so it goes. All of this is going on behind the scenes, so to speak, out of conscious awareness, as you watch your favorite show.

At that exact moment, a commercial comes on, announcing a vacation resort in the Bahamas. You would normally take no notice of that commercial; but at that split second, you are vulnerable to its allure and hungry to escape the internal pictures you've just been painting of yourself as a failure.

So, you suddenly get up from your sofa and book that Bahamas vacation; which a month later, leads you to a certain island beach; which in turn leads you to a whole new life, completely different from any you might have previously considered. And you may well never know what happened!

This is how we end up in the Bahamas, or working as an astrophysicist, or married. Maybe we get lucky and end up in the right place. Or, like millions of people who are unaware of these interactions among their dynamic succession of thoughts and feelings, their places of attention, and all those stimulations from the outside world, maybe you end up in a quite unfortunate place.

If, however, you've created the brave new mind that I'm suggesting you create, one that brings serene readiness to every moment, then you will be much less vulnerable to a random television commercial or to any random stimulus.

This better awareness would sound something like the following. "I seem to be suddenly and strangely open to this idea of a Caribbean vacation, and that surprises me. I have so much work to do to make my business a moneymaker—

doesn't a vacation at this precise moment sound like a luxury, and maybe even like self-sabotage? I wonder why I'm so open to this random idea?"

Even better would be: "I'm very aware that I've been pestering myself just out of conscious awareness about how poorly my business is going and how down I feel about myself. So, of course, the Bahamas are bound to sound enormously attractive. But I haven't earned that vacation, and my business can't afford my taking that vacation. Now, of course, I am entitled to it—I am certainly entitled to vacations. But not at this split second, and not because a commercial popped onto the screen!"

The serene readiness I'm describing is in part exactly this: the way that you quietly, calmly, and serenely monitor that chaotic corridor full of bumping thoughts and feelings; not idly, just to watch them pass by (as a meditation practice might invite you to do), but at the ready, just as our hall monitor or boxing referee stands ready.

You are calm as you do this (and I'll explain that state in a moment). And you are prepared, to take our example, to notice that some complicated interaction between that dynamic succession and a television commercial almost sent you to the Bahamas rather than back to minding your new business, where you know you belong.

Chapter 12

When You Need a Lot of Neurons

Flow and the issue of safety

Let's return to our hall monitor for a moment.

He is paying attention to the goings-on in the corridor, while at the same time working on his math homework. Now, say that a moment arrives when he has the sense that the answer to his math problem is very close, but he needs to apply his full attention to the problem or he won't be able to solve it. What then?

In order to get the silence that he needs and so as to get as many neurons as possible working on the answer, he decides to step into an empty classroom where it is peaceful and serene. In that safe, silent place, he works on his problem, and given the attention he is paying to it, likely solves it.

Moments like these are pivotal moments for the tens of millions of people who find themselves needing to use their whole brain in the service of a creative project, a difficult calculation, or anything that needs intense focus and mental attention.

Too many people can't achieve this state, which is colloquially called *flow*. They can't get their neurons to release their grip on whatever those neurons are currently doing and join together to think deeply. As a result, their novel doesn't get written, their scientific theory isn't born, and the problems these people are trying to solve go unsolved.

For that hall monitor to enter that quiet classroom and get on with solving his math problem, it has to feel safe to him to leave the corridor unattended. If it doesn't feel safe to leave the corridor unattended, he will not have internal permission to step away, and as a result, he will not be able to concentrate sufficiently on the problem at hand.

What is the result of not being able to step away? First, he will feel frustrated, disappointed, and maybe even furious that he is stuck in the corridor and not able to pay full attention to his math problem. Second, the math problem will not get solved. Third, this will result in a bad grade, with all the repercussions that come with bad grades. Many negative consequences will likely result from the fact that it did not feel safe to leave the corridor unattended.

To get lost in flow, which is absolutely required if you are to innovate, create, solve problems, and otherwise use your full brain power, you need to have a basic trust that it is safe not to pay attention to anything else, including both the outside world of distractions and the inner world of dynamic succession.

This coveted sense of safety is connected with the serenity you are hoping to achieve. The more you feel safe allowing that dynamic succession to go by largely unmonitored— because you trust that it will not incline you toward despair, nor create unnecessary anxiety or develop terrible cravings, and so on—the more serene the internal atmosphere you create for yourself.

Several billion of your eighty-six billion neurons will still be engaged in that dynamic succession of thoughts and feelings. That is always a part of your brain's repertoire of activities. But if you can achieve this sense of safety, most of your neurons will be available to fix that plot problem in your novel, dream up the right marketing strategy for your business, or craft the right thing to say to your angry teenager.

This dynamic succession of your thoughts and feelings needs your monitoring, both because you want to be aware of its trajectory and because you want to influence it as necessary. At the same time, you are obliged to pay attention to whatever else requires your attention, whether that is solving a math problem or peeling a potato. This state of divided attention is necessary in many situations.

Sometimes, however, you require more than divided attention. You want your full attention focused on a pressing matter, like the chapter you're writing or the difficult conversation you're about to have. To get that full attention, it must feel safe to leave your dynamic succession of thoughts and feelings on its own. You are still giving it a modicum of your attention, but such a small amount that whatever is going on there is neither affecting you nor distracting you.

A certain practiced sense of safety is needed in order to create or think deeply. If you do not feel safe leaving your constantly churning thoughts and feelings to the side, you will not have enough neurons available to get your thinking work done. Too many of those neurons will still be standing guard in the corridor, worried about all that pushing and shoving. As a result, little to no thinking work will be accomplished.

Chapter 13

What controls?

And what will pop out of the consciousness cupboard next?

Picture someone making breakfast. Surrounding that person, on all four walls, are many cupboards—a hundred cupboards, let's say. Behind each cupboard door, waiting to pounce or to otherwise have its presence felt, is a particular thought or feeling. Together, the contents of these cupboards make up the full repertoire of your mind's possibilities.

Behind one door is anger. Behind another is a sense of defeat. Behind yet another is the pressing desire to buy new clothes. In one cupboard, there is a warm feeling about childhood, while in another is the thought that this might be a good moment to move to another country. Behind one cupboard door is the thought that your job is overwhelming you; behind another is envy, and so on. Maybe there aren't just hundreds of these—maybe there are thousands and thousands.

Now, what controls which cupboard door will open next and allow a thought or a feeling to take center stage? It can't be the person herself. We know that a person isn't saying to herself, "Let's open the anger door now, I think I would like a little anger today." No, we are not consciously orchestrating that dynamic succession. We may be able to influence it—that is certainly our goal—but orchestrate it moment by moment? No.

Well, if it isn't the person, who or what is it? Today will surely be a day of despair if, for example, defeat gets out of its cupboard and enters our system. But who or what decides to open that cupboard door or to keep that door firmly closed? Who or what is the keeper of those cupboard doors? Who or what is writing our play? Who's in charge here?

We simply do not know. No one has solved the "hard problem" of consciousness or come close to convincingly explaining how the mind works. But certain things feel true.

First of all, it feels like the thing we call "personality" influences whether the cupboards open or not. My relatively rigid formed personality handles a lot of that dynamic succession, presenting me with pretty much the same thoughts and feelings I have always thought and felt, even going back as far as childhood. There is that mechanical aspect to the mind's activity, as it repeats itself according to its owner's formed personality. The puzzle that is *personality* connects to the puzzle that is *mind*.

Second, it feels rather as if we have laid down "unconscious" rules or principles that we demand our mind follow. A mind rule or principle might sound like "Make sure to stay skeptical —the world wants to fool you!" or "Don't take on too much, you're really not up to it!" Maybe some limited number of these rules or principles are highly influential in deciding which cupboards will open and which will never open. Influential how? We do not know.

Third must be the effects of those important experiences that still circulate in our system, those snapshot moments and pivotal events that seem to matter so disproportionately. Something may have occurred for just a split second thirty years ago. For whatever reasons, that objectively trivial but nevertheless influential occurrence, whether positive or negative, is still alive in us. That sexual failure, that bit of criticism we received, the race that we won, that second-place finish, or that dismissive look still partially control the orchestration of our cupboards. This is because of how the brain encodes experiences,.

There is much more to consider. But let's just settle into a deep understanding that our dynamic succession is subject to causal connections, just as everything is. However, dynamic succession's causes are so complex that untangling them is beyond us. We can rather count on certain thoughts and feelings reappearing, because of how our formed personality operates, how snapshot moments work, and so on; but that is not at all the same thing as being able to predict or control those thoughts and feelings.

What we can do is guess and influence. Our hall monitor, noticing that Billy and Max have that look in their eye, can guess that pushing and shoving are about to begin. And he can prove influential when it comes to preventing that shoving or stopping it once it's commenced. These are of great interest to us: our ability to guess what our mind intends to think next and our ability to influence its direction.

Chapter 14

The Story of Prime Directives

On guiding and influencing our dynamic succession

Imagine offering a simple instruction to your mind and inviting it to use that instruction "all the time" as it rolls out its dynamic succession of thoughts and feelings.

At a guess, we should probably presume that it would have to be a very simple instruction and that it would need to very accurately convey our intentions.

To take as an example one likely candidate, maybe a sound and useful primary instruction to yourself would be "Do the next right thing" (which is one I like). This suggestive, impressionistic phrase would stand for all of the following: that you want to be ethical, productive, proactive, and that what comes next is a choice that you get to make; and so on.

How might employing such a prime directive work? Very simply. You would simply say to your mind, "I want everything you do to be measured against this prime directive. Maybe you are about to whine. Is that really the next right thing to do? Maybe you're going to send me bolting angrily out the door. Is that really the next right thing for me to be thinking, feeling, and doing?" And so on.

Over time, and with any luck, your mind would actually work that way, measuring what it wants to produce or what it has produced against this sensible prime directive. The key is that it is a *prime directive*. It is *the* thing you are saying to yourself as you chat with your mind. You don't change it, doubt it, forget it, or abandon it.

I'm reminded of a time when I would take my grandson Ethan to kindergarten every morning. At a certain point, just before the door to his classroom would open, a long line of kindergarteners in early morning care would be delivered by their teacher. Every single time she released them, she would say the same thing: "Make good choices." That was her inviolable message to them.

A second anecdote comes to mind. An elementary school teacher, having encountered my ideas about the availability of multiple life purposes and the utility of life purpose statements and prime directives, took her class out to a nearby stream. There, she had them select largish, polished, river stones to bring back to the classroom.

Back at the classroom, each child chose his or her "prime directive" for the year—be nice, be kind, be friendly, etc.—and painted it onto his or her stone. The stone then sat on their desk all year, reminding them of who they wanted to be. She explained to me that she had never had a calmer, easier to manage, or more productive class in her teaching life.

Now, you might have more than one prime directive. Think of the multiple prime directives of Alcoholics Anonymous—

simple, stalwart concepts: "First things first." "One day at a time." "Easy does it." "Keep coming back." These are far more than just accessible, portable reminders. They are prime directives that together amount to a way of life. Each one does an excellent job of reminding the mind what it ought to be thinking; and together, they contribute mightily to the serene readiness we're exploring.

Imagine that you have consciously announced the instruction, "Do the next right thing." But unconsciously you hold the belief, "People are not okay, and I don't like them very much or trust them as far as I can throw them." Surely inner conflicts are coming. But imagine if you *didn't* have the instruction "Do the next right thing" in place. Wouldn't that be even worse? Good self-instructions can't guarantee hoped-for outcomes. But they must certainly improve the chances for hoped-for outcomes, mustn't they?

Chapter 15

Your Prime Directive(s)

Creating guardrails with simple
slogans

Maybe inner peacefulness matters to you, along with your career. Your priorities may also include activism, your intimate relationships, exercising your creativity, being good to yourself, your physical health, travel, using your mind, healing from past trauma, and being a responsible citizen. Maybe there are three or four others as well. These may *all* be important to you. Isn't that how life really is? Full of multiple purposes, not one single purpose?

We both need and are entitled to multiple life purposes of our own choosing. First, we require them because we do not want to fall into the trap of supposing that life has just one purpose which we are supposed to scramble after and pine over (and never find). Second, we need them because that is the truth: that many things are important to us, and that many things rise to the exalted level of life purpose choice.

At the same time, while we can and should have many life purposes, we can encapsulate something about the tone or essence of all those many life purposes into a simple life purpose statement or prime directive that we craft for ourselves. My personal life purpose statement is "Do the next right thing," and I think that might do a nice job for you, too, as a solid way of holding the essence of your multiple life purposes.

You want the prime directive or the prime directives that you choose to support two core ideas, firstly, that you are obliged to identify what's important to you, and secondly, that you must clearly communicate those decisions to your mind as directives. These directives then guide your dynamic succession of thoughts and feelings. A prime directive that supports only one of your life purposes falls a bit short of that mark since it leaves your other life purposes out in the cold. Care is therefore needed in how you word and frame your prime directives.

AA slogans like "First things first" and "One day at a time" do exactly this supportive work. Unpacking "First things first," we get: "Of the many things that are important to me, the first among them is sobriety." Unpacking "One day at a time," we get: "Even if you didn't achieve your sobriety goals yesterday, today is a new day and an opportunity for a fresh start regardless of what went before. If I keep making my best effort to live my recovery with each new day, while not beating myself up about my shortfalls, all things are possible."

The reason these slogans have worked for so many millions of people is that they do a beautiful job of supporting a person's multiple life purposes while at the same time identifying sobriety as life purpose that is the "first among many."

We are very familiar with prime directives governing all sorts of walks of life. The most famous might be, "First, do no harm," a guiding principle associated with the medical profession that is considered a fundamental ethical standard for healthcare providers. Fans of science fiction and robotics will remember Isaac Asimov's First Law of Robotics: "A robot may not harm a human being, or, through inaction, allow a human being to come to harm."

These prime directives and first principles abound, and for good reason. They encapsulate our ethical strivings, our understanding of life's priorities and what matters most to us, our sense of rightness and appropriateness, and our hopes for personal efficacy and societal well-being. They announce what we stand for.

We would not nod approvingly if, say, the medical profession's prime directive was "Always be aggressive" or "Always do what benefits pharmaceutical companies." Prime directives of that sort would not meet our ethical standards.

With regard to our personal prime directives, they provide the mind with vital guidance. They create guardrails so that our dynamic succession of thoughts and feelings doesn't run off the rails. They remind us that we must take charge of our psychological and existential reality. And they do this in the simplest way possible, through just a handful of words that become our life-organizing and life-saving instructions.

We'll return to the matter of prime directives shortly. But let's stop for a reminder.

Chapter 16

Why Now?

New minds for terrible times

Let's stop for a moment and remind ourselves why this brave new mind, one manifesting serene readiness and providing its dynamic succession of thoughts and feelings with prime directives, is needed right now.

Maybe some other kind of mind was adequate to deal with situations arising a thousand years ago, or even thirty years ago. But we are in a new time and a new place. The pressures on the individual, the species, civilization, and the planet have never been greater.

A bald list of the contemporary challenges that our current mind is presumed equal to handling doesn't capture the flavor or reality of this moment. This is true in part because some significant percentage of our troubles are cumulative.

We are weighed down by an accumulation of doubts about the goodness of the human species; doubts about the possibility of equity and justice triumphing over inequities and injustices; doubts about the possibility of erasing poverty and starvation;

doubts about the possibility of the fair distribution of wealth and resources; and doubts about the meaningfulness of our pursuits and options.

This is an accumulation. All of these doubts have existed forever. But over the past several decades, hope has faded. Reappearing fascism reduced hope; nuclear weapons reduced hope; the massive strength and venality of global entities (banks, corporations, institutions, and others) reduced hope; pervasive capitalism, with its greediness and constant noisy invasive sales tactics, reduced hope; the dispersion of families reduced hope; the hypnotic intrusiveness of the Internet, smartphones, games, artificial intelligence, and other digital genies reduced hope; and so on.

This has resulted in hopelessness by a thousand cuts. To take just one example, each of us is under constant never-before-seen attacks on our identity and our livelihood. On any given day, I receive scores of spam messages and scam efforts. Who doesn't? My website is attacked thousands of times. Whose isn't? I'm informed that one of my books is the perfect vehicle for a major motion picture (a scam), that my website is now in someone else's possession and would I like it to be ransomed back (a scam), that if I do a few easy things, I can make millions (a scam), and so on.

Human beings have always faced attack. But have we ever seen anything like this? It is one thing, and quite large and dramatic, for the Prussians to lay siege to Paris and try to starve the French into submission during the Franco-Prussian war of 1870. But it is another thing, and the epitome of death by a thousand cuts, to be bombarded by cyber threats continually. The latter does not, as the French were forced to do, demand that I eat the animals in our local zoo. But it seriously harms our mental health.

There is daily and ongoing crisis fatigue. There is the absolute conviction that we no longer have any privacy. We know that our information is flying around the globe at the speed of light. We search for something—Celtic jewelry, say—and ten seconds later, an ad appears at the next site we visit, advertising Celtic jewelry. Coincidence? Not hardly! We are all now rightly paranoid, and how is that feeling?

The list of new and current stressors is both diverse and motley in the extreme: Artificial intelligence; globalization; the erosion of empathy; hours and hours spent in a mindless trance; lost and doomed professions; trending fascism; scarcity; and the medicalization of everything. This is a strange list of apples and oranges, but taken together, they form our zeitgeist, our particular moment.

We can't divorce ourselves from it. We are obliged to deal with it. Serene readiness is the best answer, and I'll explain how and why. But let's take a moment to look these contemporary challenges right in the eye so as to cement the conviction that mind change is really needed. Where should we start? Maybe with your local shoe repair shop—oh, wait, that doesn't exist any longer, does it?

Chapter 17

The Shoe Shop Down the Block

On lost and vanishing professions

In the 1930's, there were 100,000 small, independent shoe repair shops in America. In 2024, there were 3100. We see the same declines for watch repair shops, for tailors, for furniture repair shops, for upholstery shops, for bookbinders, for camera repair shops, for milliners, for sign painters.

We know why, of course. These declines reflect broad societal shifts toward convenience, automation, mass production, and disposable goods, alongside the loss of traditional apprenticeship pathways and skilled crafts education. Some of these trades are seeing niche revivals as part of the slow-living and maker movements, but in the main, these are dying breeds.

A young person here and there might decide to opt to pursue one of these trades or crafts. But if he did, it would almost certainly be for lifestyle and philosophical reasons, say because he wanted to participate in the sustainability movement. He would be swimming decidedly against the stream, facing not only difficulty but scorn. Shoemaker? Really?

Now, you may not be considering becoming a shoemaker or a tailor. The fact that these professions are vanishing may not concern you much. But what about writer? Visual artist? College professor? Anthropologist? Actor? Physicist? How will artificial intelligence affect the professions of the musician, therapist, or coach? Will tenure continue to exist? Will universities continue to exist? Will teachers still teach, or will AI provide all manner of routine instruction? What is coming?

It may not matter to you that cashiers and bank tellers will disappear. But it may matter to you a lot that your own cherished profession is seeing the handwriting on the wall. Whole professions, ways of life, and walks of life are vanishing, and these include professions that matter to us a lot. We have never come close to imagining a time when the professions of writer, teacher, artist, or musician might vanish. That time is here or coming.

You likely didn't have your heart set on becoming a postal worker, an assembly line worker, a data entry clerk, or a farmer. The loss of those professions may not register much. But consider: All those folks will be looking for work. The whole world of displaced workers, persons who can no longer do what they were doing, will be looking for work. That is the epitome of competition.

Not only are you obliged to deal with what may prove to be a dramatically changing and changed landscape, but you will be eyeing your next move alongside millions of other eyeballs eying their next move. Where maybe there might have been a handful of applicants for a newly-minted job, soon there may be hundreds and thousands. Your brave new mind will have to deal with that.

This is all new. We've had colleges around for 1,500 years and teachers teaching for thousands of years. But is a college degree going to continue to be relevant? Enrollment has been declining for years. Costs have been spiraling upward. The logic of graduating with a degree in English, a sociology, or art is proving less tenable all the time. Is the "traditional professor" soon to become a dinosaur, after thousands of years of grace, prestige, and security? This may be coming— and the mind will have to deal with it.

The brave new mind we are picturing will have to be brave in its understanding of such widespread cultural changes. It must make sense of such changes, prepare for them, navigate them when they arrive, and face all that chaos and disruption serenely, or else be overwhelmed by it. You may not notice that the shoe shop down the block just shuttered its doors. But you will notice with horror when your profession is no longer wanted or needed. The readiness we are examining is readiness for exactly that.

Chapter 18

Our Version of Soma

Street drugs and the medicalization
of everything

In Aldous Huxley's *Brave New World*, "soma" is the powerful, state-sanctioned drug that plays a central role in maintaining societal order and individual happiness.

Soma is described as a substance that provides a euphoric, hallucinogenic escape without any significant side effects like hangovers or long-term health issues. It is heavily distributed by the World State as a means to control the population, ensuring compliance, social harmony, and avoidance of discomfort or dissent.

Whenever individuals feel anxious, unhappy, or conflicted, they are encouraged to take soma to dissolve their negative emotions and achieve instant tranquility. It is famously referred to as having "all the advantages of Christianity and alcohol and none of their defects," underscoring its dual function as both a spiritual and recreational sedative.

Soma reinforces the World State's philosophy of "Community, Identity, Stability" by stifling individuality and the natural human experience of suffering. Soma serves as a beautifully chilling metaphor for how pleasure and distraction can be weaponized to maintain control, raising powerful questions about the balance between happiness, individuality, and societal stability.

Well, we are not exactly there in our brave new place. We are, however, in a related place. On the one hand, we have massive addiction and enormous reliance on street drugs and prescription drugs for getting us through the day. This is not overtly state-sanctioned, to be sure, and in that regard, there is no official soma. What there is, though, is the state-sanctioned medicalization of just about everything.

From the medicalization of obesity to the medicalization of doing a school task slowly to the medicalization of rich folks' worries, as a society, we are on the threshold of considering every human discomfort a medical problem. Medicine, on balance, is a good thing—even a great thing. But the medicalization of every aspect of living is another matter. To compound matters, medicalization's stakeholders are among the most powerful and influential folks on the planet.

To take just one aspect of the destructiveness of the medicalization of everything, our mental health is surely one of the worldwide issues confronting us. Person after person feels the rug of civilization being pulled out from under them. And if we are completely wrongheaded when we act as if this deteriorating mental health is a medical issue, then where are we? We are facing the doom that will attach to everything human being treated as a drug opportunity.

In the last seventy-five years, psychiatry has supported the view that what we are discussing in this book—the stresses affecting the contemporary mind—are not implicated in our human experience of despair. There is no despair—there is only the "mental disorder of depression," which, so they say, is a medical matter to be treated with chemicals. This point of view is so entrenched that all the human words that we have previously used to describe sadness, including the word sadness itself, have been functionally removed from our vocabulary.

The contemporary person half-senses what is happening. She knows that what is going on around her and inside of her must be implicated in how she feels and that her suffering must be related to, say, the fact that her profession has vanished. Yet the psychiatrist she decides to visit will appear to be 100 percent uninterested in her circumstances or her predicament. Isn't this bizarre disconnect itself crazy-making?

Why the medicalization of everything has happened is easy to understand. In addition to the obvious ways in which the profit motive and professional creep have played their roles, its main cause is the same cause that killed off existentialism. Existentialism demanded that human beings take personal responsibility wherever personal responsibility could be taken—and human beings balked. The species could not tolerate setting the bar that high.

People have largely done this medicalization of everything to themselves. They have deeply consented. At the same time, they know that something is wrong with this picture. As we remind ourselves why a brave new mind is required, let us remind ourselves of a single reality: One version of soma is already here, in the form of psychiatric medication, and it isn't making us happy.

Chapter 19

Poverty, Scarcity, and the Shrinking Middle Class

The terrible trends that pressure
the mind

That famous anecdote from the French Revolution where a highhanded, aristocratic woman, when informed that the peasants had no bread to eat, replied, "Then let them eat brioche" (which for English speakers got translated as, "Then let them eat cake"), could not be more pertinent today. She lost her head; and we are losing our minds.

Our contemporary mind is obliged to replace that outdated image of the upward spiral—the hopeful icon of progress and possibility, with its slogan, "the American dream" and visions of a robust, ever-growing, middle class—with harsh reality. Poverty is growing. 3.5 billion people earn seven dollars a day or less. Scarcity is growing. Birth rates are shrinking (meaning fewer workers to keep the ship of civilization afloat). The middle class is shrinking.

We had our idealizations, romantic notions, and mental models. You know them; white picket fences, two-car garages, or maybe a high-ceilinged Manhattan loft; carefree living and Fourth of July barbecues. There are Bohemian versions of the dream of the good life: a small Paris studio, croissants, and affairs with existentialists. We've had our happy-place mental models. Yours might not have looked like mine, but we each had a dream and a sense of possibility. We did not see a world trending toward horror.

Now it's housing crises and world inflation, water shortages and energy shortfalls, climate degradation and environmental collapse. All of that is on our mind, in the foreground or in the background. If you have children, you are worried for your children. If you have grandchildren, you are worried for your grandchildren.

These trends disturb the mind. You personally may have water, but when you hear that Mexico City has officially run out of water, that affects your mind. That is another one of the thousand cuts causing despair. Against your will, you notice that in one year, 2020, the global middle class shrank by 90 million people. Well, that trend will surely reverse itself, the pundits say. But are you feeling optimistic?

It hardly matters if any one of these trends is affecting you personally. The very fact that these are the trends disturbs the mind. It is one thing to see the house down the block double in price just as you were thinking about shedding your apartment and entering the house-hunting market. It is another thing, and disturbing in its own right, to notice that absurd doubling even if you aren't currently hoping to buy. The very fact that all of this turbulence and churning is going on, even if it doesn't affect you personally, grinds at you.

What sorts of trends and turbulences? Here are some:

Wage stagnation
Inflation and rising costs
The widening gulf between low-paying jobs and high-paying jobs
Automation and technological change
Regressive tax policies favoring the rich
The erosion of social safety nets
The decline of unions and the precariousness of employment
The expensiveness of urban centers
Aging workers trying to adapt to new industries

These all feel like runaway trains. How soon will this train or that train run right off the rails? And these trending disasters inevitably bring with them the kind of resentment, discontent, and unbridled anger that give would-be authoritarian leaders a toehold, and then a foothold, and then a grip. That is clearly happening. We are obliged to go to that awful place next.

Chapter 20
Trending Fascism
The rats have returned to enlighten us again

One of the most prescient paragraphs in literature is the last paragraph of Albert Camus' *The Plague*, his allegory of World War II, where rats are stand-ins for fascists.

Camus concludes his novel as follows:

> "He [Dr. Rieux, the narrator] knew what those jubilant crowds did not know but could have learned from books: that the plague bacillus never dies or disappears for good; that it can lie dormant for years and years in furniture and linen-chests; that it bides its time in bedrooms, cellars, trunks, and bookshelves; and that perhaps the day would come when, for the bane and the enlightening of men, it would rouse up its rats again and send them forth to die in a happy city."

We foolishly had the idea that fascism was a thing of the past, that it had died with Hitler, and that democracy and its institutions had nothing to worry about from those old, dead ghosts.

We could not have been more wrong. Fascism always returns, because according to the pundits, as many as a quarter of the members of our species are authoritarian by nature; and that authoritarianism surfaces and plays itself out as fascism.

The concern that societies, including democratic ones, might be trending toward fascism has been a topic of discussion among political scientists, historians, commentators, and just about everyone else. It is impossible not to be perturbed by this terrible trend. As fascistic rhetoric escalates, as institutions crumble, as leaders lash out at their own people, we stand in horror and disbelief. Can this be happening?

Yes, it is happening.

We see it wherever we look—the erosion of the norms of democracy:

Attacks on free elections
Gerrymandering and voter suppression
Cults of personality
Disregard of and flat-out hatred for the rule of law
Nationalism, populism, and "us vs them" rhetoric
The mythologizing of decline
Assaults on a free press
Criminalization of protest
Glorification of violence
Collusive corporate-governmental alliances
Scapegoating of minorities

Manipulation of public education
Censorship of art and thought
Weaponizing religion and morality

Each of these attacks disturbs the mind and tightens the stomach. How could trending fascism, trending despair, and trending anxiety not run apace together? It is horrible to have to live under a tyrant's thumb, horrible, inglorious, and frightening. How many suicides must be numbered among the 30,000,000 souls who, through famine, purges, forced labor, and other forms of state violence, died at Stalin's Hands? Minds are not meant to survive such terrors.

Having to live under the thumb of tyrants is nothing new. Two thousand years ago, we had Nero, Caligula, Qin Shu Huang, and Phalaris. A thousand years ago, we had King John, whose cruelties provoked the Magna Carta into existence. Five hundred years ago, we had Vlad the Impaler, Ivan the Terrible, Henry VIII, and Louis XIV. In our last century, we have had Hitler, Stalin, Franco, and Mussolini. These are just some of the headliners on a list that stretches across the continents and the millennia.

Terribly naively, we thought that was all in the past. It is not. Can we possibly face this worsening reality with anything like serenity and anything like readiness? Well, what likely won't work is trying to run away, as we may manage to run from fascism only to drop into its arms wherever we've landed.

Can an answer be to never alight, to just keep running? We have a fascinating contemporary mental model of a version of that running, the mental model of the digital nomad. Is that perhaps an answer—or its own new disturbance? Let's go there next, as we try to paint as accurate a picture as we can of what currently ails us.

Chapter 21

Digital Nomads as Mental Model

Keeping our mind on the run

Doesn't the reality of growing fascism invite the following question? Maybe the solution to it, and to the other problems that we're examining, is to keep moving?

Maybe if you refuse to align with any particular country, maybe if you identify yourself as a citizen of the world, as someone who is grabbing the best that the world has to offer, and maybe if you picture yourself as a moving target rather than as a stationary one, that might be a kind of answer?

That is to say, is being a digital nomad a kind of answer? Is that merely a romantic illusion or a half-hearted survival tactic, or is it an excellent way to organize a contemporary life and a modern mind? Istanbul for a month; Quito for three months; some cheap, beautiful place for the winter. Will that work, practically and psychologically?

There appear to be about 40,000,000 digital nomads worldwide, with more hitting the road all the time. And how many folks are functionally digital nomads? Maybe they haven't left home, but they are operating in that new around-the-clock way, with no real boundaries, no intimate relationships, no sustaining identity, and no solid center.

Being a digital nomad can sound romantic: Travel where you like, avoid Big Brother, earn an income from technology, and do what you love (or at least like). But just as the reality of hordes of tourists can make some romantic city completely unromantic, the reality of a life on the road may fall far short of its romantic ideal. And who or what does that life turn you into?

There was a time when a working person either ran a business or was employed by a business. Now millions of people see themselves—or have been forced to see themselves—*as* a business. They are not anything in particular but rather an agglomeration of side hustles. On the credit side, there's increased autonomy (of a sort), the freedom to set your own schedule, the lure and reality of adventure and novelty, and a sort of sense of community via coworking spaces and online chat forums. That's the upside.

On the debit side are loneliness and isolation, the disruption of long-term relationships, and feelings of disconnection. Besides these emotional dimensions, there is also the stress of constantly changing environments, the additional stress of practicalities (visas, housing, internet connections, and so forth), a lack of stability, problems with sleep and diet, language barriers and "culture fatigue," as well as the challenge of establishing a work-life balance, not to mention a loss of identity, place, and family.

Which side of the ledger wins?

Well, that isn't actually our question. Our question isn't whether becoming a digital nomad is a good idea or not, whether it is a viable response to encroaching fascism, or whether it is a real solution to the problem of impending psychological collapse. Rather, our question is, what is the availability of that mental model doing to the mind? Isn't its availability itself a strange, new, additional pressure?

Few people in past generations, or in all of human history, could picture themselves merrily roaming the earth as a way of life. They might dream of moving from their village to the big city, or they might find themselves fleeing their poor country for a more affluent one. But who could picture themselves roaming the world freely? Maybe Bedouins and other nomadic peoples. But the concept of merry *individuals* wasn't a generally available mental model.

Now it is, and that produces its own stress. The fact that it is possible to picture just packing up and going makes the center hold even less. Our brave new mind, with its serene readiness, must stand serenely ready to deal with this sudden desire to divorce itself from its history, its family, its group identity—from everything, sling on a backpack, get that laptop charged, and head off for the cheapest place in the world with an internet connection.

Yes, we may not leap up and actually go. But the fact that such a notion is circulating in our brain is its own real disturbance. That we might be able to just tear up our roots and run away increases our sense of rootlessness. It is a real part of the problem that we can picture ourselves waking up tomorrow in some jungle hut, our internet café just down the dirt road and waiting.

Chapter 22
Retreat into Mindless Trance

The pursuit of oblivion, one screen at a time

There is really nowhere to run. So, what do people do to combat their current challenges and to reduce the impact of their contemporary stressors, if running isn't an option? Well, many millions find relief in mindless trance, the mindless trance associated with staring at screens.

Just as any apocalyptic futurist might have predicted, the world is drifting further and further into mindless trance. This amounts to a retreat from thinking, from feeling, from connecting, and from taking action. The boy on his bed playing video games is the future of us all, if we don't acquire the brave new mind I'm describing.

The allure of trance is just too great—virtually everyone is either on the precipice of plummeting into the rabbit hole of text messages, five-second videos, and computer games, or else has already fallen prey to their siren call. It is far beyond mere screen addiction. Trance has become our way of life. Who is present nowadays? Picture any environment: a subway train full of passengers, a business party, five teenage girls at the yogurt shop. Who isn't on his or her phone?

Mindless trance is soothing, silencing, distracting, and ultimately, unsafe. Say that one of your prime directives is "Do the next right thing." If you know that the next right thing is promoting your business, playing with your child, getting to your painting studio, or calling your ailing mother, then trance isn't also the next right thing. Nor can you positively influence your dynamic succession of thoughts and feelings while in trance. Trance of this sort, the very antithesis of flow, robs of us the chance to do the next right thing.

If your dynamic succession of thoughts and feelings is trending toward despair, and you are playing a video game in part so as to not know that it is trending that way, then two things will be true. You will be further along the path to despair after playing that video game; and playing that video game was not the next right thing to do.

Yes, the experience of trance is typically one of relief and pleasure. But pleasures of this sort do not meet our psychological and emotional needs. Rather, they lead us into oblivion.

In *Brave New World*, Huxley paints a picture of a world where tyrants rule by providing the trance of pleasure rather than by instilling fear. Sex, consumer goods, the drug soma: People are so docile and happy, so busy buying and discarding goods, self-medicating, sleeping around, and enjoying themselves, that they create no problems for their masters.

Trained to fulfill the functions of the caste into which they are born, the citizens of Huxley's *Brave New World* have been trained never to go deep. Superficiality is the regime's guiding principle. Relationships are engineered to be shallow, as citizens are taught that "everybody belongs to everybody else." Promiscuity, instant gratification, and the suppression of deep emotional connections are normalized. These two are taught hand in hand: trance and superficiality.

If someone should momentarily feel dissatisfied by all this superficiality and trance, there is always the drug soma. As the Director of Hatcheries and Conditioning, Mustafa Mond, explains during a tour for students:

"And if ever, by some unlucky chance, anything unpleasant should somehow happen, why, there's always soma to give you a holiday from the facts. There's always soma, to calm your anger, to reconcile you to your enemies, to make you patient and long-suffering. In the past, you could only accomplish these things by making a great effort and after years of hard moral training. Now, you swallow two or three half-gram tablets, and there you are."

The availability of trance as a method of control and the astounding takeover of trance states as the primary way we avoid noticing our circumstances can only be combatted by our commitment to avoiding its lure. We must stand ready not to dive down these rabbit holes, even though they now fill the landscape.

Chapter 23

On Declining Empathy

People are caring less—and we
know it

One of the hallmarks of our current situation is the new lack of empathy that we are experiencing. It has always been a fact that we had it in us not to empathize with others: Turks versus Armenians, Protestant Irish versus Catholic Irish, Jews versus Palestinians, Montagues versus Capulets—the list is endless. Our species is brilliant at holding grudges. But something new has been added to the mix.

We have been trained to care less by the manipulative forces that are served by our lack of empathy. Let's take just one example: the action movie. The action movie is a particular sort of manipulation. The typical set-up is that one man or one woman can implausibly triumph over a cadre of evildoers. A set piece of such movies is the car chase. What is going on there?

We are manipulated into identifying with the hero or antihero who is trying to escape from his pursuers. In the course of that chase, countless innocent people are killed or injured. And we don't care. We don't empathize with them in the slightest. We care about them as little as we care about deaths in a video game. All we want is for our hero to get away, even if that destroys whole families right and left.

In a 2010 study, Dr. Sara Konrath analyzed data from nearly 14,000 American college students. It revealed a significant decrease in self-reported empathy over three decades. The most pronounced decline occurred after 2000, with a 40% reduction in empathy levels compared to students in the late 1970s.

Scores on empathic concern (the ability to feel compassion for others) and perspective-taking (the ability to understand others' viewpoints) showed significant declines, particularly after 2000. The decline in empathic concern came in at 48%, while perspective-taking dropped by about 34%.

We can point many fingers as to why this has happened:

The cult of individual success versus collective well-being
The overvaluing of material wealth
The rise of digital communication
The reduction of face-to-face communication
Political polarization and a growing us-versus-them mentality
Desensitization from constant exposure to the news
Feelings of emotional disconnection in the face of global suffering
Busy lifestyles that leave little room for human interactions
More virtual reality and less real reality
The consequence-free violence of video games
Chronic stress
A culture of narcissism

And this trend is nowhere truer than among our professional classes, where we might have hoped that training and education might increase, rather than reduce, empathy. But studies focusing on medical students, for instance, have observed a decline in empathy during clinical training years. Research indicates that empathy levels tend to decrease as medical students progress through medical school—an effect only in part due to increased stress and workload.

The demanding nature of medical education often leads to burnout, leaving students emotionally exhausted and less able to connect with patients. Additionally, the emphasis on technical knowledge and diagnostic efficiency can overshadow the importance of emotional connection. Clinical training environments may also model detachment, inadvertently teaching students to suppress their emotional responses to cope with the stress of patient care.

And when they become full-fledged doctors, empathy can wane even further. There is solid evidence suggesting that empathy is declining among doctors. Studies and surveys over the past few decades have highlighted this trend, particularly as healthcare systems become more complex and demanding. Patient satisfaction surveys likewise reflect perceptions of declining empathy in physician interactions.

Again, we can identify the reasons: the increasing focus on productivity, heavy workloads, administrative burdens, and so on. The main point is that it is happening—and we know that it is happening.

This knowledge disturbs us. Like the other unavoidable truths that our mind must now deal with, truths about climate degradation, scarcity, the return of fascism, and so on, there is this truth, that people are more and more deeply not caring about one another. It is hurting us to realize the extent to which people may not care about us—and we may not care about them. This is not pleasant knowledge.

Our contemporary mind is not handling this sad news well. It would be lovely to see empathy increase all around us, and within us, too, and maybe that will happen. But for now, we must deal with what is. Is some brusque, careless interaction coming? You bet it is. And if our brave new mind is in place and working, we will stand completely unsurprised by it and serenely ready to experience it.

Chapter 24
The Collapse of Others
On emotional contagion and stress transmission

If your husband or wife is down in the dumps, how happy can you be? If everyone at work hates being there, how helpful is that to your state of mind? Cultivating your own brave new mind is an excellent thing—but how will it feel if everyone around you is struggling? Picture refugees fleeing a war zone. Aren't all of them in the same emotional boat, each one as anxious, frightened, and distraught as the next? Isn't what they are feeling "contagious"?

The perspective that individual emotional distress is worsened by the distress of those around us is rooted in the concepts of emotional contagion and interpersonal stress transmission. Emotional contagion refers to the subconscious "catching" of emotions from others, where an individual's mood and emotional state are influenced by the behaviors and emotions of the people around them. Interpersonal stress transmission occurs when one person's stress or emotional challenges directly or indirectly affect others in their social network.

Crowds at concerts and sports events share heightened emotional states. A leader's emotional tone can significantly affect team morale and productivity. Emotions expressed online spread through comments, posts, and interactions. Our mirror neurons do their part to help us mimic, understand, and empathize with the feelings of others. All of this is going on quite unconsciously, whether we are sitting with a friend, trapped in a business meeting, or rooting at a football game. We are sharing positives—and lots of negatives.

The findings of contemporary studies support what is obvious enough, that we are affected by the moods and mental status of the people with whom we live, work, and come into contact. If, as all the numbers show, and for all the reasons that we've been discussing, we are in the middle of anxiety, addiction, and despair epidemics, then we are bound to come into contact with more and more people who are struggling emotionally, including folks in our own family.

To take one example, consider the level of despair among psychiatrists. Doctors are already twice as likely to commit suicide than members of the general population. Psychiatrists have among the highest suicide rates of all doctors. The usual explanations are that they work in high-stress environments, that they find it hard to ask for care and fear being stigmatized if they look weak or unwell, that they have easier access to lethal means than do other medical professionals, and that they tend to work in greater isolation than do other doctors.

There is also the reasonable wonder as to whether they fully believe in their profession and their particular professional tool kit of chemicals, restraints, electroshock, and incarceration. Those doubts must also factor in. But what about the most obvious conclusion, that the folks they are tasked with helping are piled high with woe and that encountering them is debilitating? Even if you are seeing patients only rather briefly, and even if you are only rushing to prescribe, what must those encounters do to you day in and day out?

Consider what a psychiatrist's working day might look like: another despairing person; another anxious person; another deteriorating person; another bereft person; another person hearing voices. Perhaps another manic person, talking a mile a minute and fleeing from whatever appears to be chasing them, before another disturbed person, blaming the doctor and the world. Is daily contact with all of that pain and turmoil really bearable?

As we wind down our look at the contemporary risks and challenges that make the switch from "ordinary mind" to "brave new mind" so vital, let us cast an eye around us at the people near us, those who interact with us, who concern us, and whom we love. If they are doing poorly, we are doing that much more poorly. And nowadays, they are doing poorly. It isn't just that the numbers say it; we know it and feel it.

Chapter 25

Aristocrats, Mountain Men, and Liberated Women

The central challenge that is human nature

Over the last several chapters, we've looked at the special challenges we face today that make a brave new mind so vital.

On top of all of those contemporary challenges, however, we have all of the usual causes of human pain and anguish. Human beings, by virtue of their nature, have always faced psychological challenges. Aristocrats have; mountain men have; liberated women have. Everyone has.

We are built to have everything we could possibly want and still feel envious and greedy. We are built to hate our neighbor because of his barking dog. We have it in us to act against our own self-interest to satisfy some warlike itch or some servile need. We have it in us to consider coming in second as losing. We have it in us to permit some inner conflict to simmer for a lifetime. We are this sort of creature.

A simple, useful way to conceptualize personality is as a three-part thing made up of original personality, formed personality, and available personality. To begin with, we come into the world already distinctly ourselves, with our unique and particular genetic instructions and natural strong points. That complex of potentialities and realities is what I'm calling our original personality.

Then we meet the world and become a more stiffened version of ourselves, that relatively consistent, coherent, everyday "me," who perhaps claims to prefer mustard to ketchup and who never says thank you. This feature of personality is "thoughtless," in the sense that it operates largely by repetition and by rote. Our formed personality is cement-like, and its rigidity helps explain why we keep repeating our mistakes, thinking the same thoughts, and resisting change.

Then there is our remaining freedom to grow, to change, and to stand ready to act intentionally. We have that freedom, each and all of us, but to a lesser or greater degree. This available personality is something like a proportion; it is more when we manifest self-awareness and a willingness to take personal responsibility, less when we defend ourselves and block out self-knowledge. That smaller or larger quantity is our available personality.

All human beings share this three-part shape. It is a very strange shape, because built right into it is essential confusion, unsteadiness, and a welter of conflicts arising from the far distant past of our species.

Maybe you are born with a love of music. Just because you love music, does that mean that you must become a musician? Maybe you are born with a heightened need for risk and novelty. Because your mind is craving the thrill of another poker game, does that mean that you must risk your rent money? You're attracted to a certain look in a stranger.

Because your mind has made an archetypal match, must you follow him or her down the block and around the corner?

In human beings, there is always something smacking up against something else. We are not simple even to ourselves, and that produces all sorts of pains and messes. How can we transcend our nature when primitive urges surge up to threaten our veneer of civilized intentions, when the success of a friend makes us envious, when the opinions we hold and the opinions our children hold cause terrible estrangements? What can we do with all this humanity?

The best we can do—and, fortunately, it is a lot—is to manifest serene readiness, that state where we are as we wish to be and act as we wish to act. In that state, we stand calmly prepared to face our challenges—the ancient ones, the constant ones, and the new ones. Without a brave new mind to deal with them, they would likely prove too much to handle. With it, we can manage. First, we need to acquire serenity. And what sort of creature is *that*?

Chapter 26
Peaceful Thoughts Abound

A short history of the concept of serenity

I hope that the marriage of serenity and readiness that I'm describing proves really valuable to you and helps you create a mind equal to these difficult times. But certainly, the concept of serenity is nothing new. Human beings have aspired to it for thousands of years, and their philosophies and religions have promoted this unlikely aspiration.

The current popularity of Stoicism, for instance, can be attributed to its focus on the idea of tranquility (*ataraxia*), with Stoics like Epictetus, Seneca, and Marcus Aurelius emphasizing the importance of emotional equanimity. This equanimity was to be achieved through rational thinking, an acceptance of the natural order, and control over one's reactions to external events. The Stoics taught that serenity could be achieved through a close alignment with nature and a clear focus on what is and isn't within our power to control.

The concept of serenity was likewise central to Epicurean philosophy. Epicurus taught that freedom from disturbance (*ataraxia*) and pain (*aponia*) were the highest goods. Serenity was to be achieved by limiting desires, avoiding unnecessary fears (like the fear of death), and cultivating simple pleasures.

In Buddhism, the twin goals of inner peace and detachment were to be achieved through mindfulness, meditation, the cessation of suffering acquired through an understanding of the Four Noble Truths, and the practice of following the Eightfold Path.

Serenity is likewise a central theme in Hindu philosophy and yogic practice. The *Bhagavad Gita* teaches detachment from the results of actions and equanimity in the face of life's dualities (e.g., pleasure and pain). Serenity, in this view, is seen as a state of union with the divine (*samadhi*).

In Islamic thought, serenity, or *sakinah*, represents a state of divine tranquility bestowed upon believers who trust in Allah and submit to His will. It is often associated with moments of spiritual clarity and reassurance during prayer and contemplative reflection.

In Christianity, serenity became associated with spiritual surrender and trust in God. The "Serenity Prayer," attributed to Reinhold Niebuhr in the 20th century, echoes Christian themes of acceptance, courage, and wisdom.

Early Christian mystics like St. Augustine emphasized inner peace through faith and divine grace. In the Abrahamic religions of Christianity, Islam, and Judaism, prayer was seen as a way to connect with the divine, find guidance, release burdens, and achieve serenity. Monks and nuns embraced unencumbered, minimalist ways of life organized around contemplative practices meant to cultivate simplicity.

Renaissance humanists like Michel de Montaigne viewed serenity as an outcome of self-awareness and moderation, blending classical and Christian ideals. Eighteenth Century Enlightenment thinkers emphasized reason and self-discipline as pathways to serenity. Philosophers like Immanuel Kant advocated for a serene life grounded in moral duty and rational autonomy. Later Romantic thinkers linked serenity to nature, sublime emotions, and the primacy of subjective experiences of peace.

Taoism encouraged following the natural flow of life (the Tao) and letting go of desires that disturb inner peace. Serenity was to be achieved through non-action (*wu wei*), a concept of effortless alignment with the world.

In the Protestant traditions, examples of these efforts toward serenity have included the monastic vows of poverty and the minimalist lifestyles of the Shakers and the Amish.

Ancient Chinese practices meant to cultivate serenity include the practices of Qi Gong and Tai Chi, which focus on cultivating life energy (*qi*) through gentle movements and breathwork and are often practiced in serene outdoor settings for maximum effect.

Serenity as a concept threads its way through human history and has been practiced and cultivated by individual seekers for thousands of years. It has a distinct universal sound to it, captured beautifully in the following poem by the great Chinese poet Tu Fu, who lived in the Tang Dynasty during the eighth century.

Central to this time period was the An Lushan Rebellion, a decade-long cataclysmic event that led to a tremendous loss of life, the destruction of countless cities and towns, and a massive decline in prosperity. At the height of this cataclysm, Tu Fu wrote:

Quiet Night Thoughts
Silence in the lonely mountain,
No sign of human sound.
Yet the echo of voices
Carries through the empty air.
The moonlight fills my courtyard,
Reflecting all around.
In this quiet, my heart is still,
Peaceful thoughts abound.

This might well do as our essential definition of serenity: Peaceful thoughts abound. And why is this so important? Let's start with the body.

Chapter 27

Serenity and the Body

Less pain, better sleep, and fresh neurons

Why all this fuss about serenity? First of all, because achieving it serves the body wondrously well.

Serenity is a hallmark of psychological well-being and a key component of a workable life philosophy. But it is also something the body needs. Physiologically, serenity does all of the following:

Serenity lowers cortisol levels, reducing wear and tear on the body that is associated with chronic stress.

Serenity supports balanced adrenal function, preventing over-activation of our fight-or-flight response.

Serenity slows our heart rate, reducing strain on our cardiovascular system.

Serenity decreases blood pressure and helps maintain healthy blood pressure levels, reducing the risk of hypertension and heart disease.

Serenity bolsters the immune system, leading to a reduced likelihood of illness.

Serenity serves as an anti-inflammatory and helps regulate inflammatory responses in the body.

Serenity promotes parasympathetic "rest and digest" activity, improving nutrient absorption and reducing issues like indigestion and irritable bowel syndrome (IBS).

Serenity relaxes muscles and muscle tension, improving mobility and reducing pain. This reduced tension also supports better posture and movement efficiency.

Serenity improves neurotransmitter balance and boosts levels of serotonin, dopamine, and GABA, which promote feelings of well-being and mental clarity.

Serenity supports the growth of new neurons and the brain's ability to adapt, aiding memory and learning.

Serenity promotes deeper, more restorative sleep by reducing nighttime stress and anxiety.

Serenity reduces disruptions to hormonal systems caused by stress, improving functions like metabolism and reproductive health.

Serenity activates endogenous painkillers such as endorphins and decreases the brain's perception of pain.

Take sleep. The relationship between serenity and better sleep is well-documented. Achieving a state of calmness and peace can significantly enhance both the quality and duration of sleep.

High cortisol levels—associated with stress and anxiety—can disrupt the natural sleep-wake cycle, and serenity lowers cortisol, helping the body transition into a relaxed state conducive to sleep. Serenity activates the parasympathetic nervous system, which slows the heart rate and promotes relaxation.

This physiological shift makes it easier for the body to prepare for restful sleep. Serenity increases levels of GABA (gamma-aminobutyric acid), a neurotransmitter that quiets the brain, and serotonin, a precursor to melatonin, the hormone that regulates sleep. It also reduces disruptions to the circadian rhythm caused by stress, producing a calm state that signals to the brain that it is time to rest.

Or take pain. The relationship between serenity and pain management is becoming increasingly recognized in the scientific literature. The state of calm, balance, and inner peace known as serenity plays a vital role in reducing the perception of pain and improving overall pain management.

Serenity activates the parasympathetic nervous system, which decreases muscle tension, calms the nervous system, and interrupts the pain-stress cycle. It likewise counteracts catastrophic thinking, a common psychological response to chronic pain that amplifies suffering. The resulting calm and balanced mindset helps patients reinterpret pain sensations.

And what about the creation of new neurons and general brain health? Serenity positively influences the brain's ability to produce new neurons, a process known as neurogenesis, acting particularly in the hippocampus, a region involved in learning, memory, and emotional regulation.

Elevated levels of cortisol inhibit the creation of new neurons, and serenity reduces cortisol levels. Serenity likewise enhances the production of BDNF, a protein crucial for the survival and growth of new neurons, for the differentiation of neurons, and for synaptic plasticity, which enables better communication between neurons.

Remember all that better sleep? That in itself is critical for neurogenesis and the creation of new neurons. During deep sleep, the brain repairs and regenerates, fostering the growth of new neurons. At the same time, serenity is reducing cortisol levels and the other stress hormones that inhibit neurogenesis. Last but not least, serenity enhances brain plasticity and neurogenesis by creating a neurochemical environment rich in dopamine and serotonin.

Serenity is not just a philosophical nicety or some lofty spiritual principle. It is what your body wants. To not be serene is to cheat your body. Serenity is not a luxury but exactly what your body ordered.

Chapter 28
Ordering Up Serenity

We can feel it, but can we explain it?

Serenity can be exquisitely hard to achieve and may not even be particularly natural. It may be rather more natural for members of our species to live on high alert, conflicted and unsettled, with our thoughts roiling and our motives clashing, than to live serenely. But while it may be hard, or more than hard, to achieve, it is really very easy to define.

Or so it would seem.

The general definition of "serenity" is that it is a state of calmness and tranquility, free from stress or agitation. It is the peaceful mental and emotional state that each of us has experienced here and there, maybe for five minutes on vacation while sitting at a café watching the fishing boats leave for the morning, maybe for a full hour after a half-day spa treatment, maybe for a split second for no discernible reason.

Spiritual traditions tend to define serenity in terms of alignment: They often declare that serenity is the state you achieve when you are in right or full alignment with the divine, with universal energy, with God, with something or someone that is the provider of inner harmony. You are serene because you are in right relationship, and serenity is a gift of grace.

Psychological definitions emphasize ideas like effective stress management and emotional regulation, the absence of emotional turbulence, and the resolution of inner conflicts. Serenity is seen as a mental state of low arousal and positive emotion marked by feelings of safety and relief that you have worked to achieve. You are serene because, for example, you've finally resolved that long-standing conflict with your parents and are now content in your own skin.

Social and cultural definitions of serenity emphasize the idea of collective calm, for instance, the sense of calm experienced during moments of ritual, celebration, or shared silence. In this view, serenity is the fruit of sharing and connected to unity. Personal serenity arises from the embrace of community.

Philosophies and religions have their various ways of defining serenity. A Stoic would emphasize accepting life's circumstances without attachment to outcomes. A Buddhist would see it as a state of inner stillness and detachment, one that is achieved through mindfulness and meditation and that is a step toward enlightenment and freedom from suffering.

A Christian would likely define it as a gift of peace bestowed by a higher power, often described as "the peace that surpasses understanding." In Eastern religions, serenity is regularly conceptualized as alignment of one's energy to the universal flow, achieved through practices like yoga, Qi Gong, and contemplation.

In the world of romantic literature, serenity is a poetic quietude of the heart and mind, often compared to a still lake or a clear blue sky, that embodies a sense of grace and ease. In the world of art, serenity is an aesthetic of simplicity and balance, for instance, in a painting, an object, or a piece of music that evokes a sense of peace and clarity and that is often described as visual or auditory tranquility.

Related are natural and environmental definitions, where serenity is seen as the feeling of peace and harmony experienced in natural settings like forests, mountains, or beaches. Serenity, in this view, is a certain sort of connection to the soothing rhythms of the earth, one that is "simply available" to anyone who ventures into nature.

Taken together, these definitions are actually more confusing than clarifying and more in conflict with one another than in alignment. Is it enough to walk in nature to experience serenity, is it that readily available? Or can it only be achieved through a lifetime of contemplation or a regimen of self-awareness and personal growth? Is it more something that we achieve or more something that can only be received as a kind of spiritual gift? And so on.

Maybe the truth of the matter is that we each know what serenity feels like, but as to where it comes from, how to achieve it, how to experience it for more than a moment, or what to do when and if it vanishes...well, there are confronted by some contentiousness. So, where shall we land?

Chapter 29
Four-Legged Stool
Regarding serenity's sturdy base

My grandfather on my mother's side worked in New York's Garment District a hundred years ago. I possess a few mementoes from his time in the garment industry, among them a small, sturdy, four-legged stool. I don't know how he used it or what function it served, but I love having it.

Let us imagine that the serenity we are after is like that four-legged stool, as solid as can be and supported by the following four sturdy legs: a pertinent philosophy of life; a wise psychology of life; artful self-relationship; and a tool kit for self-support.

Why a pertinent philosophy of life? Because it is empowering to live according to your own understanding of life. Living that way is the very essence of authenticity and helps you align your actions with your beliefs. Developing your own philosophy of life requires self-awareness and critical thinking, and so the very process helps you understand yourself more clearly and deeply.

You get to say, "This is how I see life. I am entitled to my own understanding of how our species works, how society works, and how the universe works. I get to decide how I want to comport myself, what I can and can't expect from life, what I choose to value, where I want to pay attention and where I don't, and so on. All of that is up to me to decide."

Isn't that splendid? And powerful? Now, that isn't an announcement that may make you feel all that serene. In fact, it may make you anxious to realize that not only do you get to do all that decision-making, but that you *must* decide all those things; and that you must do so even if where you land causes you to butt heads with others. That doesn't sound like a peaceful landing place! But ultimately, it is. Once you sigh and settle into the role of sole arbiter of your personal philosophy of life, the first leg of your sturdy stool is firmly in place.

The second, third, and fourth legs are also needed. The second leg is a wise psychology of life. Life is a psychological affair, full of inner conflicts, secret motives, powerful wishes and wants, strange dreams, and every manner of thing that the word "psychology" connotes. Too many philosophies of life do not take human nature into account, and that is not a mistake we intend to make. The better you understand our tumultuous species, the better prepared you will be to stand unsurprised when the effects of yet another human foible or folly come your way.

The third leg, as crucial as the first two, is artful self-relationship. Strangely enough, most people do not position themselves on their own side. Imagine not wanting to be a member of your own team! And yet people regularly stake out that sad position. They doubt themselves; they demean themselves; they disempower themselves. The why of this is rather on the mysterious side, but they do. And how much serenity is possible if the first person you choose to badmouth is you?

The fourth leg is the possession of a tool kit for self-support. For now, let's identify just one possible tool: guided visualizations. Imagine that you regularly picture yourself as ready for something—ready to give a powerful speech, ready to share a hard truth with a loved one, ready to sit down and work on your screenplay—rather than unready to meet such demands. Wouldn't such picturing relax you a little, up the odds that you'd be able to live your life purposes, and maybe even put a smile on your face?

With these four legs in place—a philosophy of life, a psychology of life, positive self-relationship, and a tool kit for self-support—serenity has a chance. Yes, only a chance; serenity can't be guaranteed, any more than attending AA meetings guarantees sobriety. But they may make all the difference.

Chapter 30
The Zen of Zen

What sort of creature is a "philosophy of life"?

What does a "philosophy of life" look like? Let's spend a few moments taking in the guiding principles of one particular philosophy of life, Zen Buddhism.

My objective is not to teach Zen Buddhism in seven hundred words or to suggest that it is the best or most useful philosophy of life. Rather, it's to provide you with a sense of what one coherent set of principles looks like.

Here are some essential Zen Buddhist ideas:

1. Compassion (*Karuna*). "Compassion" means cultivating a deep sense of empathy and concern for the suffering of others and acting to alleviate that suffering.

2. Patience (*Kshanti*). "Patience" involves developing the ability to endure difficulties and delays without becoming agitated, while at the same time recognizing that growth and change take time.

3. Mindfulness (*Sati*). "Mindfulness" refers to being fully present and attentive in the moment, observing thoughts and feelings without attachment or judgment.

4. Nonattachment (*Aparigraha*). "Nonattachment" is the idea of letting go of desires and material possessions in order to achieve a state of inner freedom and peace.

5. Simplicity (*Kanso*). "Simplicity" refers to embracing a minimalist lifestyle, reducing distractions, and focusing on what is essential.

6. Impermanence (*Anicca*). "Impermanence" is the recognition that all things are transient and ever-changing and that we should accept this natural flow of life and thereby reduce our suffering.

7. Beginner's Mind (*Shoshin*). The idea of "beginner's mind" is approaching life with openness, eagerness, and a lack of preconceptions, even when studying at an advanced level.

8. Interconnectedness (*Pratityasamutpada*). "Interconnectedness" is the invitation to see all beings and phenomena as interconnected and interdependent, a realization that can foster compassion and empathy.

9. Discipline (*Shila*). "Discipline" connects the idea of self-control with ideas of ethical conduct, morality, and virtue by asserting that considered action is a key to personal development, spiritual progress, and moral conduct.

10. Contentment (*Santosha*). "Contentment" refers to the idea that it is possible to find satisfaction and peace within oneself, irrespective of external circumstances.

11. No-Mind (*Mushin*). "No-mind" refers to a mental state where the mind is free from thoughts of anger, fear, ego, and distractions, allowing one to act naturally and spontaneously without hesitation.

12. Presence (*Ikigai*). "Presence" is a concept that translates as "a reason for being" or "a reason to wake up in the morning." It is often interpreted as the intersection of what you love, what you are good at, what the world needs, and what you can be paid for.

13. Humility (*Kenkyo*). "Humility" refers to what in Buddhism is considered a fundamental virtue: the state of being humble, unassuming, and respectful towards others.

14. Equanimity (*Upekkha*). "Equanimity" is a term used in Buddhist philosophy that translates as "even-mindedness" or "impartiality;" it is one of the four *Brahmaviharas* (sublime states or divine abodes).

15. Silence (*Seijaku*). "Silence" refers to valuing stillness as a means to cultivate inner peace and clarity of mind in the midst of everyday noise.

16. Right Effort (*Samma Vayama*). "Right effort" refers to living life in a balanced and also wholehearted way, avoiding the extremes of laxity or excessive striving.

17. Right Livelihood (*Samma Ajiva*). "Right livelihood" means choosing a way of living and working that is ethical, that doesn't cause harm, that is beneficial to others, and that is consistent with one's spiritual values.

18. Right Understanding (*Samma Ditthi*). "Right View" or "Right Understanding" is a description of coming to a deep

understanding of the nature of reality, suffering, and the path to liberation.

19. Resilience (*Fudoshin*). "Resilience" (or "immovable mind" or "unshakable mind") refers to cultivating an unshakable spirit that remains steady and calm in the storm winds of life's adversities.

20. Loving-kindness (*Metta*). "Loving-kindness" stands for an unconditional friendliness and goodwill towards oneself and others, characterized by an unconditional, selfless love that wishes for the happiness and well-being of all beings.

Of course, this is hardly a full list of Zen Buddhist principles and practices. Another forty that are just as integral and important do come to mind. But this feels coherent, consistent, and contemporary, doesn't it? I hope this has been suggestive. This is one version of what a "philosophy of life" can look like.

Chapter 31
Stoicism Today

Why Marcus Aurelius has risen from
the grave

The ancient philosophy of Stoicism has seen a remarkable
resurgence in our century. Born in a world falling apart, having
been invented in Athens just a few decades after Alexander
the Great's conquests and subsequent premature death
upended the Greek world, it rapidly spread its wings to
ancient Rome. Then it went dormant as the Abrahamic
religions took hold—that is, when God appeared.

Stoicism appeals to us today because it articulates a way of life
that feels coherent, contemporary, psychologically sophisticated,
and morally relevant. First, it announces that we are obliged to get
a grip on our mind and that our suffering arises less according to
our circumstances and more according to how we frame what is
happening to us. This is an ancient idea...and also a modern one.

Many Stoic concepts align with the principles found in
modern psychology, particularly in cognitive-behavioral
therapy (CBT). For example, the Stoic practice of cognitive
reframing, where individuals reinterpret their thoughts to

change their emotional responses, mirrors techniques regularly used in CBT. This approach's core concepts—that we can get a grip on our mind, communicate with it, aim it, educate it, and entertain a relationship with it—are very modern ideas, yet they feel directly descended from Stoicism.

Stoicism also features related concepts of personal responsibility and freedom, putting Stoicism squarely in the existential tradition. Stoicism emphasizes personal agency and self-improvement, and followers are encouraged to focus on what they can control, rather than worrying about external factors beyond their influence. We are free to take notice of what is going on around us, and we are also free not to take notice of what surrounds us and at liberty not to engage with every random occurrence. This empowerment appeals to individuals seeking to take charge of their lives and wanting to cultivate a sense of autonomy.

If we think of service as an offering and servility as a demand, then it is fair to say that the Abrahamic religions preach servility rather than service. God commands and demands, as opposed to inviting and offering. The very idea of a bible laying down commandments that must be followed is anathema to the modern mind. Stoicism, in vivid contrast, preaches independence. Its emphasis on personal responsibility, resilience, and inner tranquility resonates with folks looking to navigate the complexities of modern life.

How do these ideas sound in Stoicism? Here's the tiniest taste:

Marcus Aurelius: "*You have power over your mind—not outside events. Realize this, and you will find strength.*"

Epictetus: *"Freedom is the only worthy goal in life. It is won by disregarding things that lie beyond our control."*

Seneca: *"Freedom is the prize we are working for: not being a slave to anything—not to compulsion, not to chance events; treating Fortune as though it were someone else's concern."*

Stoicism's anti-materialistic bent is another element with great appeal to the modern person tired of the blandishments of relentlessly expanding enterprise and frightened by the consequences of late-stage capitalism. In a consumer-driven society where material possessions are often equated with happiness, Stoicism offers an alternative perspective.

Its emphasis on virtue, character development, and inner peace suggests that true fulfillment comes from within rather than from external sources. This is a message that people are hungry to hear today, even if they can't resist purchasing the next shiny object our materialistic culture is hawking. Our brave new mind is obliged to deal with the realities of global capitalism, and Stoicism's rejection of materialism is something we may crave.

Despite originating in ancient Greece and Rome, Stoicism addresses timeless human concerns such as mortality, relationships, ethics, meaning, and purpose in ways that feel up-to-date. Its teachings remain more than relevant—they feel life-saving. I've chosen Stoicism and Zen Buddhism to spotlight because they strike me as the most psychologically rich and true to life philosophies around.

But, of course, both of these are "someone else's" philosophy; ready-made, to be sure, but also second-hand. Much more

pertinent to you is your own personal philosophy of life. And...
what might that be?

Chapter 32

What Do You Believe?

Stepping back for a bird's-eye view

No gods are invoked in either Zen Buddhism or Stoicism. To put it another way, these are simply the ideas of other people. Buddhism is more the brainchild of one person, Siddhartha Gautama, whose ideas were then elaborated by his disciples. Stoicism is more the fruit of several fellows, among them Epictetus, Seneca, and Marcus Aurelius. But, bottom line, these are simply ideas and opinions promulgated by your fellow human beings, by folks like you and me.

This truth should give you full permission to come up with your own philosophy of life, right now, without any additional seeking or searching and without much ado. Of course, you could adopt a ready-made philosophy of life if you like, one such as Zen Buddhism or Stoicism (or Taoism, Confucianism, Hinduism, etc.). You could opt for anything from paganism to Sufism to charismatic Catholicism. But wouldn't it be better if your philosophy of life were *your* philosophy of life?

Here, for example, are a few of the things that I believe.

+ I do not have a romantic view of our species. I do not believe that we are "essentially good" or that we are "spiritual beings." I think it is really very clear who we are: creatures capable of good and evil, creatures easily manipulated and quick to hate, creatures with limited empathy and lots of ego. We are who we are.

+ But I also like us, cherish us, and believe that we have many satisfactions available to us, including the satisfactions of showing up, loving, imagining, creating, appreciating, and standing in amazement at our best works and our most honorable efforts. To put all that simply, life has its pleasures; and they are genuinely pleasurable.

+ I prefer to be of help rather than to do harm. It isn't important to me whether I call that an orientation, a principle, a value, a choice, or something else—even a delusion. I stand by it. I feel compassion for the people who are trying to do good and trying to live righteous lives. And I feel compassion for how often they fail themselves.

+ I do not hold any romantic views about the universe, either. I do not believe in gods, enlightenment, nirvana, cosmic alignment, or anything deistic, theistic, occult, or supernatural. I do not believe that the universe is here to help me, chastise me, or do anything analogous to what human beings do. We are simply here for a while, and then we aren't. I do not experience that as "cold water thrown in my face"—I am serene about that reality.

I could continue listing and explaining. But my objective here isn't to share my complete philosophy of life. It's to model what trying to articulate a philosophy of life looks like. Of course, you might tackle articulating yours in some other way than by creating a list. But in whatever way you might decide to do it, don't you sense that it would be worth the effort?

This is not a workbook or a self-help book filled with exercises. Still, it would be wonderful if you stopped for a moment and generated a nice, robust list of the things that you believe. After you've cobbled together that list to your satisfaction, you might try asking yourself the following questions:

1. Does my philosophy of life hang together? Does it feel coherent, consistent, and contemporary?

2. Do I hold some beliefs that are up for grabs? Are there places where I'm not sure that I've made up my mind or where I still feel really conflicted? Can I perhaps make some new decisions or maybe resolve those conflicts?

3. If achieving serene readiness feels like a smart goal, does my current philosophy support that intention? Or are aspects of it in opposition? (For instance, you might believe that you must keep yourself informed about world politics, but you also know that serenity is impossible if you do. So, what actions do you take as far as limiting your exposure yourself to news, and how can you resolve such a conflict?)

That's the first leg of our sturdy stool, your philosophy of life. I hope that you will come to understand yours and feel confident that you have landed on your true beliefs. And of course, it would be good if it was informed by a deep, rich understanding of human nature. Let's go there next.

Chapter 33

Nine Reasons Why

Lobbying for a personal philosophy
of life

That there is value in possessing a self-created personal philosophy of life goes without saying. But it may be rewarding for us to name the many reasons why this is so. Here are nine of them.

Please go a little slowly as you encounter these nine reasons, since each speaks to a challenge that may be confronting you. I would love the idea of a "personal philosophy of life" to make sense to you, so take your time with these.

Having a self-created philosophy of life is important for all of the following nine reasons (and for more reasons too, of course):

1. Clarity and Direction. Your personal philosophy of life acts as a compass, helping you make decisions that align with your values and goals and helping prevent you from feeling lost or aimless, especially during challenging times. You could endlessly wander around a dense forest; or you could consult

your map and compass and make it to a warm inn where a blazing fire is waiting.

2. Authenticity. A philosophy that you create yourself reflects your unique experiences, beliefs, and priorities. It allows you to live authentically, rather than conforming to societal norms or the expectations of others. That we opt to live authentically is rather more important to us than that we live cheerfully. Adopting a personal philosophy of life is a powerful way to make that announcement.

3. Resilience. When life gets tough, a well-thought-out philosophy provides a framework for understanding adversity and making sense of it on your own terms. This fosters emotional resilience and helps you refocus and return to your life purposes. We are obliged to bounce back again and again; indeed, shouldn't that be one of our prime directives?

4. Personal Growth. Developing a personal philosophy of life requires introspection and critical thinking. This process helps you understand yourself more deeply, including helping you acquire a better understanding of your values, your strengths, and your areas for improvement (which I fondly call your "personality upgrades").

5. Alignment with Your Actions. A self-created philosophy of life helps you bridge the gap between what you believe and how you act. It encourages integrity by ensuring your decisions are consistent with your core principles. Imagine having as one of your prime directives, "If it matters, I take action." Wouldn't that energize you every day?

6. Adaptability. If your philosophy of life includes the (true) ideas that life is dynamic, that our life purposes can and do

shift and reprioritize themselves, and that we are obliged to be ready (*serenely* ready) for these changes and this shifting, then you are much better equipped to deal with life's vagaries and ups and downs. Your formed personality keeps you stiff; your philosophy of life can counter that stiffness by fostering flexibility and nimbleness.

7. Empowerment and Serenity. Creating your own personal philosophy of existence empowers you to take control of your life. It moves you from passively reacting to circumstances to proactively shaping your reality. It likewise helps you understand what you can't hope to control; and these two taken together, knowing what you can control and knowing what you can't control, are a cornerstone of serenity.

8. Improved Relationships. When you have clarity about your values and beliefs, you communicate better and interact with others more honestly and effectively. This strengthens those relationships that are worth having by fostering mutual understanding and respect. Want fewer misunderstandings, conflicts, and shadowy interactions? Craft a philosophy of life that supports that goal.

9. Making Meaning and Announcing Purpose. A personal philosophy of life encourages you to reflect on what truly matters to you. By aligning your life with your values, by identifying your multiple life purposes, and by living them, you are likely to produce the subjective psychological experience of meaning and increase your sense of personal pride.

I doubt that you need convincing on this score in any case. But this brief list may make it clearer why the effort to organize your beliefs into a coherent philosophy of life is worth the effort. Unfortunately, there is no step-by-step way to do this organizing. It would be stellar if this were a straightforward or effortless task, but it isn't. Are you serenely ready for it?

Chapter 34

Your Psychology of Life

Gaining insight into our weird
species

We are both conscious creatures and psychological creatures.

To ask, for example, "Is AI conscious?" is a different question from asking "Can AI be jealous?" or whether it can hold a grudge. The first question takes us down the road of "What is consciousness?" and what it means to have felt experiences. The other questions aim us in the direction of human nature and the peculiarities of our particular species.

To say that one leg of our four-legged stool is a robust understanding of the psychology of life is to announce that you have the job of understanding how human psychology works. Of course, we have accumulated billions of words on that subject. What can a person do with that welter of ideas and opinions? Well, to begin with, stay calm—serenity first. Let's calmly acknowledge that there is no single right answer here, just our reasonable efforts at self-understanding.

Second, we might do a little investigating into the various schools of thought on who we are. Let's start by looking at

Sigmund Freud, probably the most influential pundit on what makes us tick. Freud didn't explicitly define "serenity" as a psychological concept, but his work on the structure of the psyche, on mental health, and on the goals of psychoanalysis provide insights into how he might have conceptualized it.

Serenity, in a Freudian framework, could be understood as a state where an individual achieves a harmonious balance among the competing forces of the id (the primitive part of the psyche), the ego (the rational part of the psyche), and the superego (the rule-bound, punitive part of the psyche) that make up the three-part structure of the psyche as Freud saw it.

This harmonious balance would first of all require a resolution of internal conflicts. Freud believed that unresolved inner conflicts, often rooted in repressed memories or unconscious desires, create tension and anxiety. Psychoanalysis aimed to bring these unconscious conflicts into conscious awareness, allowing individuals to confront and resolve them, thereby achieving a state of mental calmness.

Freud linked psychological health to the idea of "maturity," which in his definition involves the ability to tolerate ambiguity, delay gratification, and accept the limits imposed by reality (including what he termed the "ineluctable fact of death"). Serenity might thus be seen as a mature state of accepting the tensions and limitations inherent in life.

Interesting, too, is his idea of sublimation. Freud described sublimation as the process of channeling unacceptable impulses into socially acceptable or creative activities. Serenity could arise when an individual successfully redirected their energy into meaningful pursuits that satisfied unconscious drives in a constructive way.

Freud also argued that the ego's ability to operate based on the "reality principle"—the ego's ability to postpone immediate gratification in favor of long-term well-being—contributed to serenity. This is in contrast to the id's pleasure principle, which seeks instant gratification, and which, while a powerful force, could be tamed by the ego. As Freud memorably put it, "Where id was, there ego shall be."

Freud's ultimate aim for psychoanalysis was to help individuals move from a state of neurotic suffering to what he called "ordinary human unhappiness." While this might seem like a modest goal, it implies a significant reduction in internal conflict, potentially paving the way for a much more serene existence.

Other Freudian ideas also resonate. I'm particularly fond of his notions around ego defenses, notions that strike me as true. We are defensive creatures. Just encountering a list of ego defenses is provocative: denial, rationalization, repression, compensation, fantasy, undoing, projection, suppression...we employ all of these to protect our ego from uncomfortable knowledge and painful reality.

Freud's is one vision of who we are. What, if anything, would you like to take away from this vision to add to your psychology of life? Is there a prime directive or two to take with you? For example, you could adopt "I can live with ordinary human unhappiness" or "I can redirect my energies toward my life purposes." Imagine building your own psychology of life. Is there anything from Freud to include?

Chapter 35

Developed...or Undeveloped?

Jung's distinct vision of who we are

Carl Jung, Freud's chief rival for "psychological supremacy," held views radically different from Freud's.

Their main difference is a profound one. Freud believed that we developed through various stages, a progression during which folks could (and often did) get trapped, with their "energies cathected" and their neuroses on display.

Jung, by contrast, believed that we progressively diminish: that we start life whole, and then, pressured by living and the need to adapt, begin to lose parts of ourselves so that we become more and more inauthentic and less and less our true selves. This shrinking of the psyche culminates in a "midlife crisis," when we find ourselves unrecognizable to ourselves, having lost so much of our authenticity through living.

This is a fascinating difference and distinction. I suspect that both visions hold a lot of truth to them and can even be held simultaneously. Certainly, the idea of physical and intellectual milestones makes sense. A child can't read until he or she learns how to read. Human beings are often not ready to tackle some physical or intellectual feat until they reach a certain point in their lives.

We also sense the logic of positing psychological development. Adults on average throw fewer tantrums than do two-year-olds; and if an adult regularly throws tantrums, we are inclined to call him immature (and some other things, too). We sense at least some truth to the logic of psychological maturation, and psychologist Erik Erikson's stages of psychosocial development make intuitive sense.

At the same time, it does seem to me that we are "whole" at birth—this matches up with my ideas about original personality. I think that not only do we feel like somebody as soon as we can form ideas of "me" and "them," I think that we fundamentally are somebody already, somebody with—as odd as this is to say—a complete worldview, even at the age of four.

Many fascinating Jungian ideas flow from the basic position that we are already ourselves at birth. To take one fanciful example that plays on Jung's ideas of anima and animus, what will happen to you if you fall in love with a blonde but you are programmed to find only brunettes attractive? Sound ludicrous? I'm not so sure. And if dynamics like these are our human lot, how will we factor them into our psychology of life?

Back to serenity: Jung conceptualized serenity as a state of inner harmony, self-realization, and wholeness achieved through the process of what he called "individuation." He believed that serenity arose from the integration of the conscious and unconscious aspects of the psyche, as well as alignment with a deeper, transcendent sense of self. Serenity, he argued, is the result of resolving internal conflicts and reconciling opposites within the psyche, allowing for a sense of completeness and inner peace.

Both Jung and Freud were keen on the idea that a chief psychological goal of the human project is effectively resolving internal conflicts. For Freud, conflicts arose when the id (the primitive part) and the ego (the rational part) did battle. For Jung, conflicts arose because our inner "shadow" repressed important aspects of the self, including aspects of the self we ourselves believe to be undesirable.

For both, inner life was characterized by confrontation. For Jung, we could count on confrontations between archetypal introversion and extroversion, between reason and emotion, between our masculine and feminine energies, and between a whole army of other internal combatants.

According to Jung, if you aligned yourself with the collective unconscious—that shared reservoir of archetypes and universal human experiences—and if you lived in alignment with your authentic self and inner calling, connected with the numinous (the divine or transcendent), faced and integrated unconscious material, and resolved inner conflicts through dialogue with oneself, well, then serenity was possible. But that is a mouthful, isn't it?

Are you ready for all that? Or for your version of all that?

What I hope you are taking away from this chapter and the preceding chapter is that those who have taken a deep look at our species and at human nature, folks like Jung and Freud, delineate a dynamic, roiling inner reality that can hardly be quieted with a snap of your fingers. That is why your serenity is at stake if you don't delve into the world of psychology—the world of you—and learn from yourself how serenity can be acquired, given all that civil war in there.

Chapter 36

Points on a Map

A glancing look at the territory of psychology

Let me clarify what we are after with respect to "psychology." We want to become psychologically minded enough that we can resolve our conflicts, see through our own defenses, fathom our own motives, handle our moods, and do all of the many things that support our mental health and emotional well-being.

We want to be able to do this for obvious reasons. But we also want to be able to accomplish this because we want our serenity built on self-awareness, not on some drug-induced, culturally-induced, or personally-induced trance.

We might feel serene while high, but that is not what we are after. We might feel serene while watching a hundred hours of our favorite television show, but that is not what we are after. We might feel serene while engaging in the ceremonies of a religion that we don't believe in any longer, but that is not what we are after. We want, well, let's call it "authentic serenity." You know what I mean.

I briefly described the tasks that Freud and Jung thought had to be handled for psychologically solid serenity to be achieved. If this were an encyclopedia, we would now go through another dozen or so thinkers and tease out how each viewed the road to serenity. But this isn't an encyclopedia, and that enterprise would likely only overwhelm us. Instead, let me just provide an impressionistic feel for some of these other points of view.

Freud and Jung are exponents of what is called "depth psychology." This makes it sound as if other psychologies are shallower, and maybe that is the exact intention of anointing oneself as "deep." Be that as it may, among the many other psychologies out there are humanistic psychology, cognitive-behavioral psychology, gestalt psychology, existential psychology, positive psychology, and transpersonal psychology, and there are many more.

Whether explicit or implicit, each approach has a way of picturing both what serenity looks like and the path to achieving it. For humanistic psychology, for instance, serenity is conceptualized as a state of inner peace and harmony that emerges when individuals live authentically, fulfill their potential, and experience congruence between their true self and their lived experiences. *Fulfilling potential* is a key concept here.

Humanistic psychologists view serenity as a natural outcome of personal growth, self-actualization, and alignment with one's values and purposes. If you can manage to achieve congruence between your real self and your ideal, love yourself unconditionally, get your needs met, and make meaning, you will find serenity.

Cognitive-behavioral psychology, currently the most popular psychology, focuses on getting a grip on your mind and your actions through awareness and the formation of new habits. It is about management: managing your thoughts, emotions, and behaviors. CBT posits that irrational or distorted thoughts lead to emotional distress, and that serenity is fostered by creating positive behavioral patterns that reinforce a sense of accomplishment and joy. Techniques employed include thought blocking and thought substitution, mindfulness, breathing exercises, and relaxation training.

In cognitive-behavioral psychology, serenity is conceptualized as a manageable and achievable state that arises when individuals gain control over their cognitive and emotional processes. Serenity is cultivated through active strategies that challenge maladaptive thinking, promote emotional regulation, and encourage behaviors aligned with well-being and resilience. Serenity is not seen as the absence of stress but rather as the ability to respond to life's challenges with calmness, clarity, and purpose. CBT's key concept is *new habits*.

For the existential psychologist, serenity is achieved by embracing freedom and responsibility, accepting that life is a product of our choices as well as our circumstances, and realizing that authentic living arises from confronting and reconciling the fundamental challenges and anxieties of human existence. It is not about avoiding or eliminating existential anxiety but about developing an authentic response to life's inherent uncertainties, limitations, and ambiguities. For the existential psychologist, serenity is not the absence of fear but the ability to act and find peace in the face of fear. *Serenity as an act of courage* is a key concept of existential psychology.

We could go on, and I imagine you wouldn't mind that, since I suspect you're very interested in psychology. But let us stop now. Here is the headline. We are obliged to appreciate that we are psychological creatures and must reckon with our own psychological make-up if we are to achieve the serenity I'm inviting you to acquire. You can tell from this chapter and from the previous two that there are many ways of going about this reckoning. Your prime directive? "Psychology matters."

Chapter 37
Social Serenity
Group life as prize and peril

The second leg of our stool is the psychological leg; but that includes more than the personal and the individual. Whole schools of thought argue that emotional distress and a lack of serenity are not individual matters, but rather the consequence of pressing social forces, ranging from poverty to systemic prejudice to marginalization to a lack of social support to a virulent "us" versus "them" mentality.

You might find that your group supports your serenity. They believe what you believe, they ratify your actions, they bring you soup when you are sick, they stand united against perceived enemies. This of course means that you must return the favor—not rat out a fellow cop, not doubt the existence of God, not love someone you are forbidden to love—but if you return their favors, you may well find yourself swaddled in a warm blanket of (maybe only public and skin-deep) sympathy and affection.

Or you may find yourself on the outs and made more anxious, rather than less anxious, by virtue of your group associations.

Maybe your group is at war with some other group, and you harbor zero animosity toward that other group. But here you find yourself, told to kill them. Or your group demands ironclad allegiance, ritualized subservience, and an intolerable level of loyalty. If the group's leader harms you, tough. Suck it up. He's infallible and can't be questioned.

In either case—in all cases—the other human beings who make up the groups to which you belong and the groups that surround you on all sides are bound to affect your serenity.

It is common wisdom that serenity can be fostered through strong, positive social relationships. According to what is called the "buffering hypothesis," supportive social networks can reduce the impact of stress, making it easier to maintain a sense of calm. Social psychologists have found that belonging to a supportive community enhances emotional well-being and promotes serenity. Well, yes, that makes sense. But what exactly and where exactly are these "supportive communities"?

If they exist but you have to pledge allegiance to them, will that work for you? If you have to believe everything they believe, hook, line, and sinker, will that work for you? If you have to bow down to your community's leadership, will that work for you? If you have to 'see no evil, hear no evil, and speak no evil,' will that work for you? You might get social harmony, along with some version of serenity—but at what cost?

We have the desire to relate to particular individuals, especially to our friends and those we love. But we also have the desire to relate with others more generally, as a feature of what is called our pro-social nature. We are wired for social harmony, which serves the species but can also prove a trap: We may opt for the serenity of social harmony at the cost of lost freedom.

We are built for altruistic actions that contribute to the well-being of others. At the same time, we are obliged to protect ourselves from social terrors—from an array of potential threats that may include forced conformity or even enslavement. Society may sometimes provide a comforting "warm glow effect" and heighten our sense of serenity. But we must not be so naïve as to presume that the people around us are on our side; often, they aren't.

Self-Determination Theory, another social psychological construct, argues that we are obliged to satisfy three important psychological needs. They are the need for autonomy (feeling in control of our life), the need for competence (feeling effective in our actions), and the need for relatedness (feeling connected to others). This last is significantly subtle. A person can't unilaterally relate. Someone such as Alan Turing, for example, can save his nation in wartime by cracking Nazi Germany's Enigma cipher device in 1941 and still find himself persecuted as a homosexual. That is how his country showed its gratitude.

To be serenely ready means being prepared to deal with other people as they band together, whether as members of your family, as churchgoers at that church down the block (the one eager to ban books), or as fellow writers in your writing group, all of whom see you as their rival. These folks are not apparitions with no heft and no weight; they affect you constantly. With all the serenity you can muster, keep your eyes open and stand unsurprised at their antics and machinations.

Chapter 38

Socrates and You

Acquiring the habit of self-relationship

Wise self-relationship is the third leg of our serene readiness stool. But it is very difficult to chat about self-relationship without opening up that amazing can of worms, consciousness. Not only are we conscious, but we are conscious that we are conscious. And not only that, but we can chat with ourselves about ourselves, about our motives, our defenses, our shadows, about all sorts of things that are really quite surprisingly available to us.

There is a powerful exercise in gestalt therapy where a person struggling with an issue is invited to move between two chairs placed opposite one another, fully inhabiting one side of the issue when she is in one chair and fully inhabiting the other side of the issue when she is in the other chair. Maybe the issue is whether or not to divorce, whether or not to give up a stalled career in music, whether or not to leave her religion. There is no exercise in the lexicon of therapy exercises more powerful than this one.

But who makes use of this technique in their everyday life? Who regularly sets out those two chairs? Who is accustomed to moving between two neatly-positioned chairs in the mind, turning things over, inviting clarity, and consulting with himself? Who regularly pats himself on the back and whispers, "It's okay. We got this." This is not a habit that even practiced meditators acquire. The reason is because such an exercise is not about quieting the mind or allowing thoughts to pass painlessly but rather an exercise in conversation.

Self-relationship is your most important conversation. Remember our hall monitor. He is doing several things at once: He is trying to attend to his math problem; he is monitoring the hall corridor; and he is thinking about other things as well, about the pretty girl who just passed, about getting to the bathroom before his next class starts, about his summer vacation, and more. All of that is in his field of attention. It is the quality of his self-relationship and his ability to calmly chat with himself that allows him to peacefully deal with such complexity.

This ability of consciousness to observe, comment on, and chat with consciousness suggests a kind of Platonic set-up, with a wise questioner, your inner Socrates, inviting you as your own disciple to think clearly about life. We typically call this ability self-awareness or meta-consciousness. But those terms hardly capture the flavor of dialogue that characterizes self-relationship.

Those psychologies that posit the existence of subpersonalities and archetypes seem truer to life, because we sense that a lot is going on in there. If we're inclined to use scientific language, we might say that the brain's ability to reflect on consciousness likely arises from recursive loops involving the prefrontal cortex (a part of the brain responsible for self-reflection, planning, and metacognition), the default mode network (active during introspection and self-referential thinking), and so on. But archetypal language seems rather more on point.

Let us revel in the magic and mystery of consciousness and assert that our inner Socrates is completely available at all times—at the breakfast table, at the gym, at three in the morning—to chat with us, guide us, calm us down, point us in the right direction, and remind us of our prime directives. It is patient, wise, and compassionate; and it is savvy, too: adept at handling real-world tasks. It can warn, nudge, instruct—it has an excellent repertoire of gambits.

And what if you feel like you have no inner Socrates? Stay serene, even as you feel that lack and wonder to yourself how you might approach this metaphor. We'll look at several keys to wise, supportive self-relationship in the next chapter, so not to worry. Just spend a minute or two on the following pair of questions. Do you possess a fully-functioning inner Socrates who promotes quality self-relationship? And if not, what might you try in order to lure that part of you out of hiding?

Chapter 39
The Whole and Its Bits

15 keys to solid self-relationship

Excellent self-relationship is a holistic idea: You relate well to yourself, period. You are on your own side, period. You provide yourself with wise counsel, period. It is all of a piece and is one integrated whole.

But we have the modern tradition of breaking whole things into constituent bits, those bits then becoming transformed into keys, tactics, strategies, etc. So, here are fifteen "keys" to a healthy, solid self-relationship. Think about them—they paint a picture.

1. Self-compassion and forgiveness. You speak to yourself with kindness, especially in difficult moments, and maintain the prime directive of "I am human." This phrase reminds you that you will make mistakes, disappoint yourself, and perhaps act more strictly toward yourself than toward others. Be self-compassionate.

2. Emotional honesty. You acknowledge your true feelings to yourself, noticing when you're angry, envious, jealous, upset,

and so on. Denying your own emotions, repressing feelings, projecting your feelings onto others, and so on, seriously interferes with a positive self-relationship. You are adamant about being true to what you are really feeling.

3. Self-trust. You believe in your ability to navigate life's challenges, choose appropriate life purposes, take action when action is necessary, and rise to the occasion. You trust that if you don't currently know what you need to know, you are capable of learning, and if you need to change in some way, you are capable of adaptation.

4. Growth mindset. You embrace learning, see mistakes as opportunities for course correction, and stay curious about life, including your own inner life. A prime directive in support of this aspect of self-relationship is: "I can continue to grow."

5. Self-respect. You respect yourself, even if you can't quite respect a particular action you took, a thought you had, or how you spent a given day. You affirm that you are a worthy creature, you appreciate your own efforts, and out of respect, you are civil to yourself.

6. Consistent self-care. You take care of yourself with regard to rest, nourishment, pleasure, relaxation, and the other components of a healthy life. A relevant prime directive: "I care for myself."

7. Patience. You take the time to know yourself as well as the time needed to counsel yourself, and you take all the time you need to maintain a positive self-relationship. If a necessary thing is taking longer than you wish it would, you calm yourself down and stay the course.

8. Resilience. You help yourself recover from blows, just as you would help a child who has fallen dry her tears and get back on her feet. You are firm in your resolve to bounce back, even as you lend yourself a hand.

9. Healthy Boundaries. You honor your limits and say no when you need to say no. This includes saying no to yourself: no to a craving, no to your inner trickster, no to your plan for revenge, no to the darkness brewing, and no to your future mistakes you see coming.

10. Mindful Awareness. You observe your thoughts without getting lost in them (remember our hall monitor). When the dynamic procession of your thinking is heading you in an unwanted direction, you pay attention, get a grip on your mind, and guide yourself back on course.

11. Inner Nurturing. You treat yourself as you would treat a beloved friend. Friendship is an excellent analogy. You forgive a friend; you tell a friend a hard truth; and often you just hug them because there is nothing to be said.

12. Purpose and Meaning. You identify your life purposes, those areas of life that are most important to you. Similarly, you identify the experiences that have proved meaningful to you in the past. Armed with these two lists, you're better able to pay attention to your needs for purpose and meaning in your life.

13. Authenticity. You are true to yourself, even if the truth makes you feel uncomfortable. You know when you are aligned with your values and principles and when you aren't, and you have frank conversations with yourself about what to avoid and when to act.

14. Gratitude. You appreciate your strengths, your efforts, and your uniqueness. You likewise appreciate what the world has to offer and what others have to offer. You are especially grateful that self-relationship is both available and possible.

15. Sovereignty. While you understand the limits of your personal power, you nevertheless stake out the position that *you* are in charge of you and that you can create the self-relationship that you desire. You don't doubt your essential sovereignty.

To refresh our memories: Serenity arises when you have a solid, workable philosophy of life; when you are wise about your psychological realities; and when you maintain a positive, effective self-relationship. The fourth leg of our stool is the "tool kit" leg. Let's go there next.

Chapter 40

Tools for the Van

Creating your limited, workable
tool kit

Imagine that you're a plumber and you can only fill your van with a limited number of tools and supplies to take with you on calls. Maybe your garage is full to overflowing with tools and supplies, but you are obliged to leave most of them behind when you're summoned. Which will you take? The ones you use the most often and the most important ones, yes? Remember, space is at a premium.

The same principle applies with your brain and your life: Space is at a premium. Over the millennia, human beings have dreamt up countless ways to think about serenity and to achieve it. Taken together, those are the full contents of the garage. But you must limit yourself to a handful of ideas and practices if they are to prove really useful and really be available to you. Creating and using that essential tool kit is the fourth leg of our sturdy stool.

Let me list many such tools and invite you to select some that intrigue you. Investigate those you choose further. See which ones align with your values and your personality, and begin to employ them in a daily way. How many tools, exactly? Even one would be a blessing! But maybe three or four would amount to a remarkably rich tool kit?

Practice Daily Mindfulness. Take 5-10 minutes once a day to focus on your breath and/or surroundings, helping anchor you in the present moment.

Engage in Meditation. Try guided meditations, body scans, or visualization exercises to quiet your mind.

Mind-Body Practices. You might try yoga, which integrates physical postures, breathwork, and meditation, and/or Qi Gong and Tai Chi, Chinese practices that harmonize body and mind through slow, deliberate movements.

Participate in a Tradition. Specific philosophical approaches that advocate for serenity include Stoicism, Epicureanism (Epicurus argued for a life of moderate pleasure, friendship, and the absence of fear to achieve tranquility), Taoism, and the monastic traditions.

Retreat into Nature. From Thoreau's *Walden* to Japan's practice of *shinrin-yoku* (forest bathing), immersion in nature has long been seen as restorative.

Simplicity and Minimalism. Traditions like Zen Buddhism and the teachings of the Shakers in the United States emphasize uncluttered living for mental peace.

Dancing and Rhythmic Movement. Ritual dances in many cultures are seen as ways to align the body and spirit; one modern example is the Dances of Universal Peace, a Sufi-founded practice in which movement is accompanied by singing sacred phrases from many world traditions.

Physical Movement and Tradition Together. Making long spiritual journeys on foot—pilgrimages like the Camino de Santiago), or their secular equivalents—can provide time for serene reflection while walking.

Declutter Your Space. A tidy environment can reduce mental clutter. You might start with one drawer or one corner each day.

Prioritize Essentials. Focus on what truly matters to you and let go of nonessential commitments.

Create a Morning Routine. Start each day with intentional activities like stretching, journaling, or sipping tea mindfully.

Establish a Nighttime Routine. Limit screen time before bed, read something calming, or reflect on gratitude.

Practice Active Listening. Being present in conversations deepens connections, reduces misunderstandings, and avoids conflicts that threaten serenity.

Set Boundaries. Overextending yourself also threatens serenity. Decline tasks or commitments that overstretch your emotional or physical capacities.

Spend Time Outdoors. Take walks, do some gardening, or simply sit in a park to reconnect with nature's calming rhythms.

Bring Nature Inside. Keep plants in your living space for a serene atmosphere and improved air quality.

Exercise Regularly. Movement releases endorphins and helps alleviate stress.

Eat Nourishing Foods. Choose meals rich in whole foods and avoid excessive caffeine or sugar, which can disrupt serenity.

Journal. Write about your thoughts and feelings to gain clarity and release tension.

Cultivate Gratitude. Each day, note things that you're grateful for so as to shift your focus toward positivity.

Practice Letting Go. Release grudges or worries about things beyond your control.

Unplug from Technology. Schedule regular breaks from devices to focus on in-person activities or relaxation.

Reduce Noise. Use earplugs, white noise machines, or soothing music to create a quieter, more peaceful environment.

Engage in Creative Hobbies. Painting, writing, or crafting can be therapeutic and grounding.

Enjoy Moments of Solitude. Take time alone to reflect, read, or just be.

Build a Supportive Community. Surround yourself with people who uplift you and inspire you.

Care for Others. Helping others through charity, mentoring, or caregiving is a timeless path to serenity.

Here are a few additional tools that may be coming or that may be here already.

Virtual Reality (VR) Relaxation Experiences. Immersive VR environments can replicate serene settings like tranquil beaches, lush forests, or quiet mountaintops.

Biofeedback and Neurofeedback. Devices are available that monitor physiological responses (heart rate, brain waves, and more) and provide feedback to help users consciously regulate their stress levels.

Sound Therapy Using Binaural Beats. Listening to specific sound frequencies can induce relaxation and meditative states.

Light-Based Serenity Practices. Exposure to specific wavelengths of light, such as soft blue or warm amber, can induce calmness.

Aromatherapy. You might use aromatherapy guides either in books or online to design personalized scent blends that evoke calm and serenity.

Meditation. Create tailored meditation sessions based on your goals and preferences; resources are available via searching on keywords such as "how to create a guided meditation," or try out some of the many meditation videos available free online.

Serene Virtual Communities. You might participate in online spaces focused on promoting calmness, gratitude, and positive interactions.

Okay! Pick your three or four favorites and give them a try. If you like them, turn them into daily practices.

Chapter 41

Serenity Sooner Rather Than Later

An energy boost in just four words

Imagine that you are learning to drive. To begin with, you aren't ready—how could you be? You know a lot about driving in a vicarious sense: You've ridden in cars your whole life. So, the idea of driving isn't foreign or unavailable. You also "sort of know" all sorts of practical details: that you signal when changing lanes, that you slow down when the traffic in front of you slows down, and so on. But the reality of getting into traffic is bound to make you feel highly anxious.

Maybe you've studied a manual. Maybe you have a parent or an instructor there beside you. Maybe the instructor even has dual controls so that she can brake if you aren't quick enough to brake or experienced enough to know when you need to brake. All of that is helpful. But basically, there you are, essentially alone, gripping the wheel as you navigate real traffic. There is nothing you can do to change this picture, speed up the process, or spare you from errors in judgment— nothing at all.

Now, picture yourself twenty years later, driving down an uncrowded highway, listening to your favorite music, the window opened a crack to let a breeze in, with the forested landscape passing by charmingly. Could you be more serene? Picture the difference between those two experiences. You could not have imagined this feeling or this reality at sixteen when you first got behind the wheel. But here it is, and here you are.

And...does it have to be twenty years later? Aren't you tremendously more comfortable driving after just a few weeks behind the wheel? Yes, from an observer's point of view, you may still have a ton to learn. Maybe, like many youths, you are on the reckless side, too easily distracted, prone to showing off, and so on. But subjectively speaking, don't you feel much more confident than you did just one short month ago? And isn't that revealing?

It is really rather remarkable and even unbelievable progress. That kind of progress is possible and available to you. For example, people can move instantly and all of a sudden from drinking heavily to opting for recovery. It's true that doesn't happen for every person. Yes, even for that sober person, slipping and drinking heavily again is a risk. But picture that difference happening all of a sudden. It occurs all the time.

A great deal of positive energy is generated when you decide to do something sooner rather than later. For many people, their default response to tackling something they know they would like to accomplish is hoping, wishing, and waiting. They say to themselves, "I can't do it now because I'm just not in the right mood," or "That workshop I'm taking in November will jumpstart my practice." They are in the habit of putting things off, sometimes forever.

Imagine that you possessed as a life principle and a prime directive: "Sooner rather than later." This is different from "Now"—I am not expecting you to jump up and be serene a split second from now (though that would be wonderful). "Now" is quite demanding, but "Sooner rather than later" is inviting. It is a remarkably useful point of view, a valuable understanding, and an energy boost, all in one.

If you rarely feel serene, it may seem implausible that such a state is available to you "sooner rather than later" (or maybe at all). But just picture those developmental milestones that happen of their own accord. You keep falling off your bicycle— and then you ride it. You can't read—and then you can. You drive with tremendous trepidation—and then, there you are, whistling and driving with one finger.

The magical phrase: sooner rather than later. Believe in this possibility. Don't shrug it off. Include it in your philosophy of life. "Later" is the word we employ to let ourselves off the hook. "Sooner" is our declaration of freedom. Invite serene readiness into your life by declaring "sooner rather than later."

Chapter 42

Serenity as a Practice

The 12 elements of a solid daily practice

When all is said and done, our number one "tool" for acquiring serenity is practice. We live serenely by choosing serenity and then by practicing serenity.

When someone says that she maintains a spiritual practice, we have an intuitive sense of what that person means and what that practice might entail.

We envision her engaging in certain activities in a ceremonial way, whether that is lighting candles or sitting meditatively; we expect that she spends a certain amount of time every day, probably first thing each morning, formally engaged with her practice; and we picture her practice informing all aspects of her life, such that when a crisis occurs, for instance, she uses her belief set (about an afterlife, say) and her techniques (like prayer or meditation) to see her through the crisis.

Likewise, if someone tells us that he is training for a marathon, a prize fight, or a high-altitude climb, we immediately get a picture of what that includes.

We expect that he exercises every day, even on days that he doesn't want to work out; that he watches his diet and passes up the hot fudge sundaes, even though he craves them; that he visualizes success and in other ways talks himself into the right frame of mind. We picture him taking charge of his mind and his body and engaging in a goal-oriented process that naturally includes pushing himself in ways that on many days he hardly loves.

Martial artists provide us with another model. We picture their formality: the way they bow when they enter the martial arts studio and when they face an opponent before a match. We picture their intensity: the way they shout, the way they drive themselves, the way they focus on a given move and a given routine. We picture the value system by which they operate, which revolves around the honorable use of force and which sanctifies self-control, including the self-control to walk away rather than to fight.

We can picture all this. Once we think about it, we discern that every serious practice, including the serious practice of serenity, has twelve elements to it. Here they are:

1. Simplicity. Life may be complex, but our practice is simple. It is as simple as showing up.

2. Regularity. Our practice requires that we practice every day. We do not skip our practice because it is gloomy out or because we are gloomy inside. We practice every day.

3. Solemnity. We engage in our practice because it matters to us. It is meaningful; it is respectful of our self-concept; it is a primary way we show our heroism. We treat it seriously and solemnly.

4. Honesty. Our practice is nothing if we are not honest. If we skip too many days without attending to our practice, we are honest and say, "I skipped too many days."

5. Self-direction. You and you alone guide your practice. You may learn from others, but you make your own decisions. Only rarely do you look for teachers, since you are committed to learning by doing.

6. Intensity. You can do something lackadaisically, or you can do it with intensity. You can bring your full wattage to an encounter, or you can bring just a fraction of your passion and energy. Your practice demands real intensity.

7. Presence. When you come to your practice, you come to be present. You are there and not elsewhere. You aren't half-thinking about bills to be paid or half-thinking about your child's grade point average. You settle in and become present.

8. Ceremony. You add a ceremonial feel to what you do by translating your good intentions into small, studied gestures that you repeat each time you engage in your practice. Even just a small sense of ceremony can make a positive difference.

9. Joy. Our practice brings us joy because it produces a sense of personal pride. We are doing what we intend to do. A quiet sense of joy can become the background feeling of your practice.

10. Discipline. Your practice hinges on your willingness to be disciplined in this aspect of your life. You may not be well-disciplined in other aspects of your life, but you somehow find the wherewithal to be disciplined with respect to your practice.

11. Self-Trust. Bring a strong sense of belief in yourself to your practice. By honoring both yourself and your practice, over time, you earn your own trust and grow worthier of your self-trust.

12. Primacy. Many things in life are important, including your serenity practice. The important things in life are owed primacy: They ought to come first. Whether that means "first thing each day" or carries some other meaning, find the way to have your serenity practice "come first."

I hope that the above brief conversation provides you with a good sense of the elements of practice. What might your serenity practice look like?

Chapter 43

Serenity as Prime Directive

Resolving lingering doubts that
serenity matters

It is one thing not to be able to achieve serenity right now, as part of your encounter with this book. Maybe you just can't get a grip on your mind. Maybe the past harm done to you circulates in your system in some super agitating way. Maybe your nerves are frayed. Maybe you have a restless mind that generates tons of wonderful ideas, at the expense of serenity. Perhaps you just can't sit still, literally or metaphorically.

Well, all that may and can still change.

It is another thing, however, to consider serenity a pointless or unworthy goal. If you sneer at it, if you see it as absurd, if you believe it to be a steppingstone to weakness, if the very thought of it makes you feel like a patsy, then the brave new mind I'm describing is quite off the table. If you don't value serenity, if it feels alien or "not you" or too "woo-woo" or worthless, well then, there you are.

It is your choice not to value serenity and not to opt for serenity. If you choose to do that and your life works beautifully, who am I to say a word? But if you are not feeling equal to these times, if your moods are dark and your pleasures few, if the future looks dystopian, then I have a proposal for you. Try serenity.

But it certainly does make sense to be cautious about this "serenity thing." There are plenty of possible pitfalls and pratfalls. Maybe one of the following five is unconsciously gnawing at you and making you resistant to the very idea of serenity. Let's air them out, and if we can, set them aside.

1. You might have the sense that serenity leads to complacency or is just another name for complacency. Will you lose your drive to challenge injustice, take risks, or strive for personal growth if you elevate serenity to the high place of prime directive? The short answer is no, but do you agree with that? Can you set this doubt aside?

2. You might be holding the view that serenity is really an ego defense or an escape mechanism, a charming way to avoid dealing with difficult realities. Surely some people do pursue serenity as a way to put relationship conflicts, societal problems, and personal responsibilities into the dark well of oblivion. But is that always the case? No. Do you agree that we are not talking about that sort of serenity as escape hatch?

3. Maybe you worry that "too much serenity" might make you off-putting and not quite human. If someone you love is struggling and you show up with serenity, won't that look like you don't care? Won't you seem detached and unsympathetic? Again, the answer is no, not if you are serenely ready to listen, respond, comfort, and otherwise be fully present and fully human. This need not be a worry.

4. Or maybe you worry that striving for serenity will rob you of your own emotions. Will you end up repressing or suppressing anger, grief, fear, or other emotions that serve important functions like processing loss and setting good boundaries? If someone tries to remain serene in all circumstances, aren't they in danger of not working things through? Well, no. The serene readiness we are after not only allows for emotions but prepares you to handle them. Losing touch with your emotions isn't a problem.

5. Or maybe you feel that intensity is more important than serenity. Don't you need intensity to start and run your business, work daily at writing your novel, stand up for yourself against bullies, and elsewhere in life? Yes, you do. But serenity is not an energy drain or an intensity killer. You can be serene and intense at the same time, and serene readiness is itself a manifestation of intensity. There isn't a problem of conflict between serenity and intensity.

If you're harboring some doubts, I hope you can resolve them. The serene readiness I'm describing is a good thing, and I hope you can fully embrace the idea that serenity ought to be one of your prime directives.

Chapter 44

Ready for Readiness

What being prepared looks like and
means

We've looked at serenity at some length. Now, let's take a
peek at readiness.

Our brave new mind will need to be calmly ready to deal with its
own dynamic succession of thoughts and feelings. It must be
able to function as that hall monitor does, noticing what is going
on and standing ready to intervene if necessary. It may also be
solving a math problem or engaged with some other train of
thought at the same time—but it's still monitoring the hall.

It will also need to be ready to deal with whatever the world
throws at it. And that will be a lot. We've named many of those
curveballs already, from creeping fascism to whole
professions vanishing. As it deals with the world, our poised
mind remains alert and observant, but not overly vigilant. It is
experienced at dealing with its own nature and with the tasks
that come with the project of living and stands ready.

What sort of readiness do we have in mind?

Consider the following analogies.

In basketball, you are "ready" to take a shot when you are not surprised to see the ball coming your way and not afraid to shoot it. When you are passed the ball, you candidly decide whether you are in the best position to shoot or if some other player on the team is more open. If another player is more open, you pass the ball. If you are in the best position to score and it is a shot you typically can make, you take the shot.

You are "ready" for all this even when you do not currently have the ball in your hands.

Think of firefighters, EMTs, ER nurses, ER doctors, and other emergency responders. Firefighters both *are ready* to respond to emergencies and they also *do things* to get themselves ready to respond to emergencies. They train, practice, exercise, maintain their equipment, and in other ways get ready to act. At the same time, they are ready to drop everything and respond to a call.

Thus, readiness has these two parts to it: It is a state of being, and it is also a practice.

Take the productive writer. She is serene in her belief that she *can* write, serene in her understanding of the creative process, with its many ups and downs, and serene in the knowledge that she loves writing. She is ready to write.

This means the same two things as in the previous example: She is both in a state of readiness to write, so that if an idea pops into her head, she puts the laundry aside and sets down her thoughts on paper or via text editor; and she is practiced at writing, with a routine that motivates her to create most days of the week.

Consider the wise recovering alcoholic. He is ready to deal with his cravings, because in early recovery especially, he knows they are coming. He is no more surprised that a craving has struck than our basketball player is surprised that he has been passed the ball. The cravings are to be expected. Readiness means standing unsurprised by life's predictable occurrences.

Our recovering alcoholic is prepared to experience difficulty at a family event where everyone is drinking, and challenges to his resolve when he receives an email from his ex-wife demanding that he pay his alimony and child support. He does not react with surprise when these triggers occur: He expected them, he is ready for them, and he knows what to do —for instance, take himself directly to an AA meeting.

Or take the anxious performer. It would be so much easier if she were not anxious. But she is. That means that she is obliged to stand serenely ready to perform even though she is anxious. That is a strange sounding sentence, but it reflects a truth about readiness: It is a fact that we can stand ready to do something, even though we are not ready.

We may not be really ready to date, but we say to ourselves, "I'm ready for this." We may not really be ready to divorce, but we say to ourselves, "I'm ready for this." We make an announcement, adopt a position, and talk ourselves into readiness.

This is our beginning picture. Readiness is a state; it is a practice; it is a stance we take; it is a declaration we make. We stand ready—serenely ready.

Chapter 45
Ready or Not
A century of readiness concepts

The concept of "readiness" came to prominence in the 1930s in the field of early childhood education.

Psychologists and educators like Jean Piaget explored readiness for learning, emphasizing that children needed to reach specific cognitive and emotional development stages before they could effectively acquire certain skills, like the ability to read or do math. "Readiness" came to refer to a child's mental and emotional preparedness to engage in a specific task or to handle a specific situation.

Piaget proposed certain influential "stages of cognitive development," among them the sensorimotor stage (birth to two years) and the preoperational stage (two to seven years). Arnold Gesell, another important figure, introduced the idea that developmental readiness for tasks like walking, talking, or learning were necessarily tied to biological maturation. His Gesell School Readiness Test emerged as a primary tool for assessing whether a child was or wasn't prepared for formal schooling.

These educators were focused on "developmental readiness." At the same time, and going back as far as Freud, models of "psychological readiness" were being proposed. These pundits argued that each of us was at a certain stage of psychological development, and that therefore, we could only accomplish the tasks associated with that stage. Until we "changed" or "progressed" and moved onto the next stage, we couldn't be expected to handle the challenges of that next stage—challenges like, for example, intimacy or individuation. For Freud, we regularly found ourselves "arrested" at our current stage, resulting in "neurosis."

Freud presented his notion of stages: the oral stage (birth to one year); the anal stage (one to three years); the phallic stage (three to six years); the latency stage (six years to puberty); and the genital stage (puberty onward). He argued that unresolved conflicts in any one of these stages would result in fixations leading to specific personality problems in adulthood.

While these stages were associated with ages and were meant to represent literal phases of psychological, social, and sexual development, it was their metaphoric power that grabbed people's attention. Since then, you might say of someone, ""He's stuck in the oral stage, always indulging in pleasures like eating and shopping." You could now describe someone who was overly controlling or inflexible as anal-retentive or someone who was disorganized and carefree as anal-expulsive. This analogizing has entered into the vernacular.

Many other models emerged as well. Among them was Prochaska's Stages of Change Model, meant to describe the stages a person goes through in order to change his or her behavior. His stages were: pre-contemplation (of the desired change); contemplation; preparation; action; maintenance; and termination (the point when the change is fully integrated into one's personality). This robust model is still widely used in the addiction and recovery world.

Another model that emerged was psychologist Erik Erikson's highly influential Psychosocial Development Theory. He posited eight stages of psychosocial development, each marked by a particular psychological conflict that had to be resolved before a person could move on to the next stage. The stages were: trust versus mistrust (infancy); autonomy versus shame and doubt (early childhood); initiative versus guilt (preschool); industry versus inferiority (school age); identity versus role confusion (adolescence); intimacy versus isolation (young adulthood); generativity versus stagnation (middle adulthood); and integrity versus despair (late adulthood).

At the same time, the phrase "psychological readiness" began to be used to describe an individual's readiness for therapy or for medical procedures. This particular readiness included factors like motivation, emotional stability, and an accurate understanding of the individual's condition. I remember, while training as a family therapist, how often we would be reminded that someone leaving therapy did not reflect poorly on us—the person simply "wasn't ready" for therapy. "Lack of readiness" became synonymous with "resistance" and "defensiveness."

In the 1970s and 1980s, the concept of "readiness" was adapted to measure employees' readiness for organizational change and for new roles. This involved assessing their attitudes, their motivation, and their adaptability. Athletes' mental readiness for competition became a focal point in sports psychology, with an emphasis on concentration, confidence, and managing performance anxiety. Recent research has been busily examining psychological readiness for interacting with new technologies, such as virtual reality and AI systems.

In international development and education, the concept has been applied to assess communities' and individuals' readiness for changes such as adopting new educational models and new technology. With the growing emphasis on lifelong learning, developmental readiness is used to assess adults' preparedness for acquiring new skills or adapting to life transitions. We've had a hundred years of thinking on developmental readiness and psychological readiness, and we are now adding our thoughts about serene readiness to the mix.

Chapter 46

Getting Ready and Being Ready

From excellent preparedness to
real-world action

A tennis player tosses the ball in the air three times, four times. She is getting ready. Then she pauses. Now she is ready. This time, when she tosses the ball, she launches her body and strikes the ball.

Those first three or four tosses were not irrelevant. But they were not the action itself. That explosive action was potential made manifest.

It is human nature to pointedly confuse getting ready with being ready. We claim to be "getting ready" to write our novel by first reading all the novels piled up on our night table. We claim to be "getting ready" to drink less alcohol by switching from bourbon to beer.

In each such case, there may be some truth to our claim. That switch from bourbon to beer may signal that we really will drink less soon. But it is not the same thing as actually drinking less or taking ourselves to an AA meeting. It may be a necessary part of the process, but it is surely not sufficient.

Being ready to write our novel means starting it, working on it, and sticking with it. Starting it and then abandoning it quickly, long before it ought to be abandoned, means that we were not really ready to write it, only ready to start writing it.

Being ready to do a thing means not only starting a thing but sticking with the thing, and where completion is part of the process, completing the thing.

You know intuitively how often people fail to follow through on their intentions. What you know intuitively is confirmed by the numbers. For example, studies show that 80% of New Year's resolutions fail by February, with only about 9% of folks feeling successful at having kept to their resolutions by the end of the year.

Related studies have produced similar findings. Up to 50% of people fail to act on their health-related intentions, goals like exercising and dieting (and doesn't the real percentage feel even higher than that?) 20% of the population label themselves as chronic procrastinators, usually blaming their resistance on "perfectionism" (and doesn't the real percentage feel higher than that?)

World Health Organization studies indicate that up to 50% of patients fail to take their prescribed medication consistently, even when that medication is life-saving. And remember those New Year's resolutions? Studies show that 23% of folks who make such resolutions discard them within a week.

Your brave new mind is serenely ready—which means it is actually ready, not just always getting ready. "Ready" in our sense of the word means that you are doing more than contemplating, anticipating, preparing, and so on: You are taking appropriate action.

Nor does it fully count to be ready in certain areas and not in other areas, including some that may be more important—and difficult. For instance, it is outstanding that you get to your meditation practice every morning at five a.m. If you are managing to get there daily, you are clearly ready in that domain. But if you still haven't started your home business, the one that you've been contemplating starting for years, and the one that might allow you to leave your terrible day job, in that domain you are not demonstrating real readiness.

No matter how much "getting ready" you are doing there, you are only approaching the starting line and still not running that race. Serene readiness with respect to building your not-yet-existing business would include calmly identifying the first steps you need to take, taking those steps, taking the next steps after those, living with the countless ups and downs of running a business, and so on.

You might therefore like to choose as one of your prime directives the following one: "The only proof that I am ready is that I take action." If you are a firefighter and there is a fire, you do not merely stand ready. You race toward the fire. When that fire starts, you leap to your feet and switch from preparedness to appropriate action.

Chapter 47
Readiness and Release
Cultivating the firing of trigger synapses

You stand serenely ready. You are ready in many domains: You are ready to face the tasks that your new business demands, ready to do some good, ready to react only mildly to your child's tantrums, ready to make love when you and your partner get the chance, ready to work on your novel.

You are serene, but also full of many anticipations and potentialities. You are like water bubbling closer and closer to the boiling point, getting ready to become steam and move a locomotive. But too often, nothing happens.

For whatever reasons, you don't make that business call, you don't make time for your lover, you don't work on your novel, you overreact to your child's tantrum, you don't do that good thing—visit your lonely aunt in her nursing home—that you meant to do.

You were ready—really ready—but nothing. It's rather like sexual arousal without orgasm. Arousal without orgasm can be just fine. Folks who engage in sex play will tell you that a delayed orgasm is the best orgasm. But a constant diet of failed orgasms doesn't feel good.

A constant diet of "getting ready to do something in the service of your business but then not doing it" doesn't feel good. A constant diet of "getting completely prepared to work on your novel but then not showing up to the work" doesn't feel good. We are not making ourselves proud by not delivering.

Readiness without release is both unproductive and demoralizing. It runs counter to what may be one of your prime directives, that you do the next right thing. "Do the next right thing" implies that you actually *do* the next right thing, not just think about it or prepare for it. The proof is in the pudding.

What can help you move easily and flawlessly from readiness to action?

The first image or metaphor that comes to mind is that of a trigger. A gun has not fired until the trigger is pulled. But the image of guns and triggers may not appeal to you. Other images that also come to mind—like a lever being pulled, a door opening, a foot stepping on the gas, a spark igniting, or a domino tipping over—don't quite meet the mark either.

Pressing a button and flipping a switch come closer. Pulling the ripcord on a parachute is an interesting possibility. But because we are talking about the brain, let us try out the following: the metaphor of a synapse firing.

A synapse is the small gap (specifically called the synaptic cleft) between two neurons, or between a neuron and its target cell. When we say a synapse has fired, we're describing the moment when a neuron (a nerve cell in the brain or nervous system) transmits a signal to another neuron, muscle cell, or gland.

This dynamic process is central to how the nervous system functions: The firing of synapses is how your brain processes information, enabling everything from thoughts and emotions to muscle movements and sensory perception. And it all happens really fast—signals travel at speeds of up to 120 meters per second.

This is a good image for us to employ. We want the image we employ to conjure immediacy, deliberateness, and something like explosiveness, and the firing of synapses does just that.

The following sentence may sound strange to you, or it may make instant sense. "I am firing my synapses." What this sentence is meant to connote is that you possess a way to take charge of your brain action and move your mind from its excellent readiness to a different state, one where your body is moving and your intentions are being realized.

The main point is that readiness without release is not a good program. In order to support our split-second decisions to act rather than to retreat, we are on the hunt for a simple reminder that we can use tactically to move us from inaction and mere readiness to action. Try out "I am firing my synapses" or some variation on that theme.

Whatever language you land on and decide to use, that statement then becomes one of your operating instructions and your prime directives. Remember that serenity and readiness are not enough without action. The fact that the water that is nearly boiling is ready to turn into steam will not move the locomotive. We need the steam.

Chapter 48

A Shallow Dive

Analogies from the world of physics

Let's take a shallow dive into the world of physics and come back with a few analogies and maybe some food for thought.

1. Why did the water boil? Because it was ready to boil.

Materials exhibit "readiness" to change states (e.g., from liquid to gas) when they approach *critical points*, such as specific temperature and pressure thresholds. At such times, only a little more energy is needed to get "over the threshold" to the next state. Think about this. Wouldn't it be that much easier to do "x," whatever "x" is, if your atoms were already excited and "anticipating" the next step or phase? Water that is almost ready to boil is "anticipating" boiling. Can you feel that?

2. Why did the spring suddenly spring? Because it was coiled and ready.

Think of the ideas of potential energy and activation. A system is "ready" to do work when it possesses potential energy. For example, a compressed spring or an object held at a height has stored energy that can be released when the conditions allow. In chemical physics, a similar concept is the *activation energy* needed for a reaction to occur. A system is ready to undergo change once this energy threshold is met. You might think of serene readiness as coiled potential energy lightly held. Can you feel that?

3. Why did the circuit start oscillating? Because it had arrived at its natural frequency.

In phenomena involving resonance, a system (like a swing, a circuit, or a radio) is "ready" to oscillate at maximum amplitude when it is tuned to its *natural frequency*. This readiness depends on external forces aligning with the system's inherent properties. Picture that beautiful alignment —where something "outside" (say, a golden opportunity) meets your serene readiness to act. There you go, oscillating!

4. Why did the ball roll down the slope? Because nothing opposed gravity.

A physical system's readiness for motion or evolution depends on its *initial conditions* and on the presence or absence of *external forces*. For example, a ball at rest on a slope is "ready" to roll when a force like gravity is unopposed. But let's say you oppose gravity—you hold onto the ball. Then it won't roll away. Our analogy: You may have to oppose a force (like, say, the psychological doubt that you are equal to writing your novel) in order to move from serene readiness to vibrant action.

5. Is the cat alive or dead? Let's take a look!

In quantum mechanics, a *superposition state* refers to a system that simultaneously exists in multiple possible states until it is measured. Schrödinger's famous thought experiment illustrates superposition: A cat inside a box where there is a radioactive atom that could potentially poison it exists in a superposition of "alive" and "dead" states until an observer looks in on it and checks.

Our fanciful analogy: You might be existing in multiple possible states with multiple and varying levels of readiness— and then you check on your situation, your circumstances, and your intentions, and voilà, you determine to do this or that. The cat is alive! To misuse the language of physics, you move from entanglement to coherence. Isn't that an exceptional idea? You become coherent to yourself!

The above is meant to be amusing. But these are serious analogies as well. There is something about the transition from boiling water to steam that interests us. There is something about natural frequencies and resonances that suggests how readiness and circumstances might connect. And consider the simple picture of a slope and a hand holding a ball: As simple as that picture is, there is a ton to learn there about initial conditions and external forces. And who can forget Schrödinger's poor cat! I hope I haven't given you nightmares.

Chapter 49
What Is Readiness?

Conviction and practice in tandem

Readiness is the state that results from the conscious choice to meet both internal reality and external reality with candor, energy, skillfulness, and a sense of personal efficacy. You acquire this state through conviction and practice.

This readiness has an urgency and an immediacy to it. It needs to be available *right now*. You can't be ready to fight a fire three days after it has burned itself out. That's too late.

Remember that this is serene urgency and serene immediacy. You aren't on edge, you aren't overly vigilant, you aren't anxious. It is a serene urgency and a serene immediacy, but that doesn't mean it isn't an alert and heightened state. You are serene, but wide awake.

You might think of it as active stillness. This is serenity in the service of action, of adaptability, of responsiveness. It is stillness, but without a hint of passivity. It is an active rebellion against inner noise and outer noise, a rebellion for the sake of instrumental living. The demands of modern life are relentless, but we do not retreat: We stand ready.

Freud famously said, "Where id was, there ego shall be." By this, he meant that our rational faculties have the power to effectively deal with our primitive impulses. Let us play on that phrase by asserting, "Where psychology was, there philosophy shall be." That is, rather than be held hostage by some psychological experience (say, of jealousy, anger, or meaninglessness), we employ our self-created philosophy of life and our prime directives and thereby stand ready not to be enslaved by our psychology.

So, there you are, standing ready. But ready for what?

You've snapped your fingers, you've shored up your personality shortfalls, you've resolved your inner conflicts, you've met your psychological challenges, you've calmed your existential worries, and you find yourself serenely ready. Excellent! But...ready for what?

On the one hand, you are ready for "anything and everything." But you also stand serenely ready in various specific ways. For example, you may be an amateur basketball player, a professional firefighter, a New Yorker, an Irish Catholic, a father, a husband, a hobbyist furniture maker, self-diagnosed with ADHD, a civil rights activist, and a recovering alcoholic.

Each of these identities makes its own demands. In your shop space in your garage, where you do your woodworking, you stand ready to use your power tools carefully. In church, you stand ready to deal with your restlessness as you listen to the Sunday sermon, having prepared yourself for a certain amount of tedium. At your AA meeting, you get ready to share, because you know that sharing is a valuable part of the recovery process. You show up ready in these various ways, depending on the situation and the circumstances.

You stand ready in context; and you also stand ready to varying degrees. Even if basketball is your favorite pastime, it is not your whole life. You do not visit your girlfriend "as a basketball player" or shop at the market "as a basketball player." The identity of "basketball player" is not encompassing. By contrast, if you are a police officer on duty or a soldier in a war zone, such identities are much more encompassing. And it may be the case that the identity of a medical doctor or a Zen master is fully encompassing, or nearly so.

You stand ready in different ways depending on the context. You likely did not stand ready as a parent before you had children. But once a child arrives—well, that is a different situation! Then you stand ready to care for your infant continuously.

We could look at a hundred contexts and a hundred readinesses. But let's limit ourselves to roughly a dozen. Looking at these will paint a robust picture. Let's begin with Gary Cooper, about to face Ben Miller, Jack Colby, and Jim Pierce, gun-toting members of the Miller gang. Is our town marshal ready? Not hardly.

Chapter 50

High Noon

Readiness in the domain of good
and evil

There is nothing harder than being good. Oh, when it's easy, it's easy. You hold the door open for that old chap with a cane. Pretty easy. You say a friendly word to your neighbor as an expression of lovingkindness. Not too hard. You make a donation to a righteous politician. Easy-peasy.

But what if your high-paying job is as a cog in a ruthless company that is doing harm? That's not such an easy one. What if, like the marshal in *High Noon*, you are obliged to stand up to three bullies, and your town isn't behind you, and you're sweating bullets? Much less easy. What if your country is fighting an immoral war and you are drafted? Will you find the courage to say no? Not many do. What if your fellow reporters are being arrested right and left for speaking the truth? And so on.

Goodness is not easy. A serene readiness to be good can help. If you are always ready to act in the domain of good and evil, that moral readiness will allow you to take action in the moment, appraise situations from an ethical point of view, and influence your dynamic succession of thoughts and feelings in the direction of goodness. You may still balk; you may still retreat; you may still fail yourself. But you have a better chance of upholding your values if you stand ready to be moral.

How does this readiness work? First, it is a nimbleness in the moment. You see a blind person approaching an obstacle that could trip her. You stop what you are doing, leap up, and move the obstacle. You don't need praise or applause for doing this: You just do it because it is the right thing to do. In real life, most people will not leap up to take that action. Serenely ready to act morally, you do.

This moral readiness helps you instantly appraise the situations you face from an ethical point of view. Maybe you would love to paint a series of paintings employing iconography from a particular indigenous population. You can already see those paintings in your mind's eye, looking gorgeous and brilliant. If you evaluate them solely from an aesthetic point of view, you might launch right in. But if you are always alert to questions of good and evil, you might stop and wonder if this cultural appropriation is or isn't defensible. Maybe you decide that it is; and you launch into creation. And maybe you decide that it isn't; so you will have to grieve the series that can never be.

Would it be easier, common, and all too human not to bother with conducting that appraisal? Of course. But we are setting the bar high, exactly where you know it ought to be set. Set it there, and you fall for fewer traps.

Remember the famous Solomon Asch conformity experiments from the 1950s? Participants were placed in a group with ringers (actors in on the experiment). They were then shown a card with a single line on it, followed by another card with three lines of varying lengths. They were then asked to identify which of the three lines matched the length of the first line.

The confederates would intentionally choose the wrong line, giving a unanimous but incorrect answer. The true participant was often seated in the last or second-to-last position, so they heard the incorrect answers from the confederates before giving their own. Asch found that about three out of four participants conformed to the group's wrong answer, even though the correct answer was completely obvious. 75 percent of participants demonstrated this moral lapse. That is a very large number.

This serene readiness of your brave new mind will help you avoid pitfalls of this sort in the domain of good and evil. You won't plagiarize that paper, although you are tempted. You won't betray a friend even though there is a nice reward for doing so. You won't act with careless cruelty even though that is your inclination. Seeing where you are heading, you invoke your prime directive of "Do the next right thing" and do the next right thing. That may not be easy, but we are not discussing ease. We are chatting about cultivating a way of being equal to this moment and matching your intentions.

Chapter 51

Ready to Create

From reality to dream

The usual phrase is, "Turn your dreams into reality." In order to create, the opposite is true. A creative person is obliged to quiet their ordinary reality, that storm of doubts, bills, grudges, disappointments and storms on the horizon, and drift into the dreamy place called flow or the trance of working where everything vanishes. There, the universe is silent and a new poem, song, or sculpture is born.

Creating may be one of your life purposes. It certainly is for my clients in the arts, many of whom come to me complaining that they find themselves readier not to create than to create. How can that be? They say they want to paint, write, sing, compose. But they aren't painting, writing, singing, or composing. Isn't that strange?

Or maybe it is quite to be expected? Is it perhaps just much harder than people imagine to ready ourselves to dream? Does reality grip us much more firmly than we know?

Take a typical situation. A writer who loves fiction would like to write a novel. She has some ideas for a novel, but none of her ideas feel really vibrant or urgent to her. On top of that lack of vibrancy and urgency, she has a ton of doubts: She wonders whether she is equal to writing a novel; if it will be any good; whether anyone will want it; whether it will prove safe to expose her private thoughts; and if it will amount to a good use of her time, and so on.

Of course, she isn't ready. Far too much reality!

She knows what she should do. Silence her doubts. Pick an idea. Just begin. See how it goes. Trust. Take a risk. Get some words down. Show up each day, if only for a few minutes. Outline. Make some notes. Organize. See what she's wrought. Proceed. It's so simple to say. It's so straightforward.

But she just isn't ready!

Can you sense what being serenely ready to create is all about? It isn't about brilliance. Brilliance doesn't make you ready. Being ready isn't about having ideas. Blocked artists may be brimming over with ideas. It isn't a lack of courage, either. Our artist may be manifesting his courage all day long just by facing his commute and his day job. It isn't a lack of skill, patience, discipline—it isn't any of those things. Being ready in this sense means that our artist is prepared to leave the world of the known and the ordinary and venture into the unknown, where their next creation resides. Not everyone is ready for that adventure.

Reality brings with it a certain sort of stuckness. Picture our hall monitor again. He has to let go of the hubbub in the corridor, all those students bumping and pushing and chattering, for the sake of getting his math problem solved. He keeps an ear on his reality, on his job of hall monitor, but not an eye. He is not watchful. He is immersed in his math problem. If reality whispers or roars, he can come back. But he has functionally silenced reality and can devote the lion's share of his neurons to his math problem.

This shift from reality to dream is the essence of creating. If you are interested in creating, you are obliged to train your brave new mind to be ready to separate from the iron grip of reality and drift into the luxury of dreaminess. This might sound like, "I'm very ready to leave reality behind," or like, "Enough reality for one day! Let me travel to Venus for a while." It could sound like, "I really want a waking dream;" or it might just sound like the *whoosh* of silence.

Chapter 52

Entrepreneurial readiness

Standing serenely ready for the tasks of business

My coaching clients in the arts typically hate certain of their necessary tasks and roles. They only grudgingly give interviews or open up about their work. They only grudgingly send out that query email, the one asking for what they want and need. They only grudgingly read the book contract, the recording contract, or the gallery agreement that arrived a full week ago. They only grudgingly follow up on an excellent lead. Or they don't do these things at all.

If only they could stand serenely ready to put on a hat that didn't fit!

We are all scrambling in our modern times, moving from one technology to another technology, excitedly joining a social media network and dropping it a year later, rushing off to Lisbon to see if that might be the place to live, then off to Albania, then joining a startup that looks promising, then working eighty hours a week and hating it, with only the promise of making it big keeping us going, then noticing that we are ill, lonely, and demoralized, then returning to nature, wondering how to throw in the towel.

We may not have a choice: Scrambling may be the new way. The Tao of today may be upheaval, unsteadiness, confusion, quicksand, and scrambling. Whether that is precisely true for you or not, it is likely that you must regularly put on hats that do not fit comfortably: this hat demanding smarmy extroversion, that hat demanding tedious marketing, the next hat demanding a conviviality as false as a laugh track. But if you are serenely ready...

More and more people are opting to live the life of the solopreneur, or being forced to live that life so as to make ends meet. Maybe they deal in currencies. Maybe they've created a start-up tech business. Maybe they cobble together several creative pursuits, like photography, painting, and graphic design.

Maybe they sell a product or a service online, or in the alternative, from a roadside stand. Perhaps they engage in a traditional solo business such as yoga teacher, life coach, hairdresser, massage therapist, psychotherapist, dentist, or family lawyer. The list of self-employment "options" is very long.

Some hold salaried jobs that pay the rent while engaging in side hustles. Some work entirely online, and many have become digital nomads. They may work completely alone, or with a small support staff of independent contractors—a webmaster, a social media assistant, a graphic designer—who are themselves solopreneurs.

Recent statistics suggest that there are almost 600 million entrepreneurs worldwide. Many are just getting their feet wet —in the United States, for example, approximately 16.5% of adults are recent entrepreneurs, meaning that they're engaged in running a new business that is less than 3.5 years old. In low-income economies, often as much as 80% of the population is self-employed. These are large numbers!

As someone who has coached creative and performing artists for almost forty years, I know intimately how unprepared they are for doing business. A wall as thick as the Great Wall of China stands between them and even their most ordinary entrepreneurial tasks, like announcing an upcoming concert, querying a literary agent, or asking the boutique down the block to carry their line of jewelry.

A serene readiness to do business would help all these solopreneurs tremendously. If only they could get out of their own way, in psychological terms. If only they could add "doing business" to the long list of activities that support their life purposes, and that, while not meaningful in themselves, support meaning. If only they could make peace with buying and selling, even while holding their nose.

It is a long way from a lemonade stand to late-stage capitalism. But one of our prime directives is to be real. A central rationale for creating and adopting a brave new mind is that the times demand it. Right now, the times are making entrepreneurs out of hundreds of millions of us. As with everything else in life, we did not ask for this. But we are obliged to calmly face this reality and take care of business.

Chapter 53

Ready to Relate

Is authenticity the whole ballgame?

Let's create exactly three categories of relating, for the sake of discussion. They are: authentic relating, agenda relating, and persona relating.

When authentically relating, we are truthful. We say what's on our mind and reveal our intentions.

With agenda relating, we are after something. It could be getting the kids to clean their rooms or winning the battle for partner at our law firm.

In persona relating, we are speaking from our role. We are speaking as a police officer while writing a speeding ticket or speaking as a kindergarten teacher on the first day of kindergarten.

Each of these comes with subcategories and all sorts of wrinkles. And of course, these aren't the only ways that human beings relate. But these three categories capture quite a bit of reality.

It turns out that we need to stand serenely ready with regard to all three. We want each role or mode available to us, and we want to be unsurprised if we find ourselves relating in one or another of these three ways.

Maybe you pride yourself on always communicating truthfully and authentically. Well, that will make it difficult for you to hide your cards or play a role. Imagine a police officer communicating authentically at a traffic stop and saying, "I have a quota of tickets to write today. So, sorry, I'm writing you up for speeding even though you were only going five miles over the speed limit. Your bad luck!" How long would she remain a police officer? And would that even prove particularly humane, or would it be received more like an added slap in the face?

Or possibly you always have an agenda. I was watching a real estate reality television show where a couple was looking for a new home. Every single thing the husband said had an angry edge to it. Even if it was, "I don't mind the color of this wall," he sounded furious. To put it in a perhaps odd-sounding way, his agenda looked to be rage. Whether he was furious at his wife, at house-hunting, or at life, who can say? But he was clearly operating from one single agenda.

Or maybe you always relate according to your persona. Perhaps you are always "the professor of English with perfect grammar" and you never let a dangling participle go by unnoticed or unremarked. People will be quite unlikely to appreciate that. They will walk on eggshells around you, grammatically speaking. You are forcing them to triple-check the emails they send to you and maybe even not send those emails, lest they end up chastised and humiliated. Is that a good way to be?

You want role flexibility, which means that you stand ready to adopt the role that is the "right" role for that moment. Is this a moment to be open and transparent? Okay. You are ready for that—you are prepared to feel vulnerable. Is this a moment to push your agenda? Okay. You are ready for that—ready to feel assertive. Is this a moment to speak from your persona? Okay. You are ready to feel constrained and artificial.

Can you sense the different sorts of readinesses involved here? Just as we refuse to say, "There is just one purpose to life," we refuse to say, "There is just one way to relate to others." Our philosophy of life is wiser than that. Our understanding of human nature and the reality of human situations alerts us to the truth that there is more than one appropriate way to interact with others.

It would be so relaxing if you could always interact in "just one way." That would be blessedly simple. But life demands more of us than that. It demands that we stand ready to choose, often in the space of an instant, the best way to be with the person across from us. Our brave new mind is prepared to serenely engage with our fellow human beings in the wisest way possible.

Chapter 54

Sexual Readiness

On the sad story of extended celibacy

Let's spend a few minutes on the touchy subject of sex (pun intended).

Sex is supposedly natural. Presumably we know how to do it and can be expected to rather enjoy it. But has that ever really been true? And might that be even less true today? Studies suggest that 20 percent of couples engage in sex less than ten times a year and 30 percent less than twenty-five times a year. There you are, with a partner who presumably attracts you, and you make love once every two weeks, or less often than that—maybe much less.

Among singles, thirty percent of young men report extended celibacy, defined as no sex for at least a year. And that trend is growing. The numbers seem to suggest that sexual intimacy is on the decline. We could name some likely culprits, among them health concerns, chronic fatigue, career overcommitment, performance anxiety, parenting stress, and so on. But isn't something else also going on?

Mustn't one culprit surely be a lack of serene readiness for sex? If your vibe is shyness, reluctance, awkwardness, distaste, fear, or something else that is the opposite of readiness, isn't sex almost certainly off the table? And isn't that readiness exactly what is attractive: that feeling in the air that the two of you are ready for sex, that sex is imminent. Picture water boiling, ready to become steam. That water is ready to boil—and observers know it.

Now, all that excitement, anticipation, and readiness may not culminate in sex, maybe because the attractive person in question is someone you work with or the spouse of a friend, and so on. Maybe there are societal injunctions, family rules, or your own principles and reasons at play. But even if sex isn't the outcome, that readiness can and will be felt. There will be excitement in the air. And while that may prove dangerous in a given situation, it is also the spice of life.

Right now, we are in a rather sad place with regard to sex. Serene readiness would surely help, even if just for the sake of a little flirting! Feel the difference between "I'm ready" and "I'm not ready." And not just ready but serenely ready: excitement but not agitation, interest but not attachment, curiosity but not obsession, confidence, not clumsiness. There is a sense of competence rather than a sense of incompetence, a smile rather than a frown. Joy!

Your brave new mind supports sexual intimacy and erotic potency. Your serene readiness to engage in sex and to enjoy it gives off sparks that ignite sexual fantasies, sexual hunger, and sexual encounters. Just as we have mislabeled despair as depression, we have also mislabeled a lack of sexual readiness in all sorts of unfortunate ways, including as a medical issue or akin to a mental disorder. But surely that is largely off the mark. The same lack of readiness that is hampering people in all sorts of domains must be showing its face here, too.

Take erectile dysfunction. There may be medical issues involved: high blood pressure, hormonal imbalances, medication side effects, and more. There may be psychological issues involved: performance anxiety, unresolved conflicts and past traumas around sex, disabling stress, and so on. But a key must be a lack of serene readiness for sex. The lack of a brave new mind that anticipates pleasure must be a key.

Yes, we might possess all sorts of reasons for not exchanging bodily fluids with a particular person. But years of celibacy? Sexless marriages? Buckets of cold water? Isn't that just too sad? Our brave new mind invites us to revisit these ancient matters, these feelings that are as old as the species, with an updated serene readiness to participate and to enjoy.

Chapter 55
Ready to Resist

Peacefulness without appeasement

We aspire to be peaceful inside. That inner peacefulness is good for us. But inner peacefulness does not equate to outer appeasement.

There is a sense in which we must surrender to life's realties; and there is a sense in which we must resist. Resistance is an existential ideal, a human ambition, and our way of meeting our own standards and making ourselves proud. It is also a face of absurdity: the resolve that we are obliged to resist, even if what we are resisting is Goliath.

It is easy to contrive language that lets us off the hook. God resides in everyone, everyone has good in them, everything is for the best, everything happens for a reason, and other homilies and platitudes mask the harsh reality that millions of people act evilly and can only be stopped via brute force. No other historical truth is more obvious.

It is likely that your philosophy of life will include as one of its prime directives some version of your willingness to resist.

Our humanitarian ideals matter to us, ideals of civil rights, freedom of speech, freedom from religion, freedom to gather, due process, and the many other rights enumerated in documents like the Magna Carta and the Unites States Constitution.

We want these rights for ourselves, and we want these rights for others. We want fairness, equity, and justice. It is unlikely to strike you as good enough that you have a lot while others have far too little. Whether you align that prime directive with ideas like empathy, conscience, a moral sense, a "still small voice," or something else, it is likely that you will embrace that call. Which in turn means that resistance is your lot.

If you're of my generation, you will remember those horrific pictures of the self-immolation of Thích Quảng Đức, the Vietnamese Buddhist monk who set himself on fire in June of 1963 in protest against the persecution of Buddhists by the US-backed South Vietnamese government. He sat serenely in the lotus position at a busy Saigon intersection while fellow monks poured gasoline over him, then he lit himself on fire and remained still as he burned to death.

A famous photograph of that moment, taken by journalist Malcolm Browne, shocked the world and became one of the most iconic images of the 20th century. President Kennedy confessed, "No news picture in history has generated so much emotion around the world." Did his sacrifice "really" matter? Who can say. But we all understood that this was what individual resistance looked like. We had a model of resistance seared into our brain.

Let us aspire to be serenely ready for the good fight. That doesn't mean that we won't also be afraid. It is natural and reasonable to be afraid. Resistance sets the personal bar very high in the direction of risk. Maybe the best we can hope for and aim for is fearful resistance. Well, then we be serenely ready for that. We can stand serenely ready to be afraid and to resist, both.

There is another important sense of resistance. We are obliged to resist ourselves: our own cravings, our own dark thoughts, our own prospective misadventures. We need an alert system that is loud and clear, one that shouts, "Watch out!" loudly enough that we can hear it even as our dynamic succession of thoughts and feelings is careening us in a direction we do not want to go. We must resist there, too.

One of our prime directives must be "I stand serenely ready to resist." Doesn't that fill you with self-respect? Isn't that exactly aligned with your philosophy of life? Yes, that is a high bar. We understand why this is a challenge; we don't want to arm wrestle dictators. We don't even want to arm wrestle our own cravings. That is all just about too much. But listen to that prime directive: "I stand serenely ready to resist." Isn't that rather inspiring?

Chapter 56

Ready to Steward

Your brain, your child, your world

The relationship between you and your mind has the flavor of stewardship to it. Yes, you are trying to get a grip on your mind, which sounds like control. Yes, you are trying to influence the direction of your thoughts and feelings, make course corrections, and so on. But there is also a wise, gentle, loving aspect to this relationship. It is, well, rather like parenting. You are the parent to your mind.

What does a good parent do? Comfort. Instruct. Be resourceful. Act with integrity. Nurture and care. Present a vision of right action, of challenges, of hardships, of joys. Lead with gratitude and respect. Cultivate a sense of collaboration. Help work through developmental challenges and celebrate growth milestones. Strive for improvement. Filter what the child consumes, whether that's food or social media. Cultivate creativity. Minister to bruises. Set limits. Lobby for rest and a good night's sleep. Well, and love.

Imagine for a moment that the world has been taken over by a handful of tyrannical oligarchs who control everything, including the earth's water and air supply. What would you say to your child? Nothing? Would you offer up a litany of dire warnings? Whisper some instructions? Would you put resistance on the table? Find a way to provide some "absurd" hope? What would you do?

Picture that scenario. Thinking about how you might steward your child in such dire circumstances can help you picture how you might want to steward your own mind. Just as a parent is aware of the developmental challenges that are coming, like the tantrums she can expect from her two-year-old, you are psychologically wise and aware of the challenges that your mind is likely to face, from despair to cravings, from racing obsessions to sudden anxieties. You stand ready.

Stewardship has about it the idea that you consider something to be valuable. Maybe it's the ozone layer, or the river snaking through your town. Maybe it's your own integrity. Maybe it's a certain friendship. Maybe it's resistance to tyranny. Maybe it's supporting the mom-and-pop pie shop down the block. And maybe it is serenity and the readinesses we've been discussing. You take action as a steward because there are things you value.

I am sitting in a hospital waiting room as I write this. Near me is a boy of about two who is shouting, "No doctor! No touching! No doctor! No touching!" As I understand it, the boy has hurt his foot and was here yesterday for X-rays and other indignities. Of course, his mother knew that he would not want to return. She is not surprised by his tantrum, and she is as prepared as she can be to handle the situation.

She calmly tries one thing after another to soothe him and to take his mind off his impending appointment. There is the juice pouch; there is the book. There is the song she sings; there is the story she tells. There is the snack; there is another snack. There is the way that she strategically ignores him so as not to overdramatize or inflame the situation. All excellent stewardship!

"You are such a great boy," she says. "You are such a brave boy," she tells him. She is ready for this not to work. She knows that there is no guarantee that anything she tries will be able to take his mind off what's coming. But she has her tool kit of tactics, and she is calm in the face of his tantrums. She doesn't blame him, she doesn't chastise him, she doesn't mock him—really, who in his position would *want* to be there? She lovingly tries things while half-smiling.

Right stewardship of your brave new mind means caring for and cultivating your mental and emotional landscape with wisdom, discipline, and intentionality. You treat your mind as something valuable that requires conscious tending, like a garden that flourishes when nurtured but becomes overrun with weeds if neglected. You choose to value yourself; and because of that choice, you mindfully steward your thoughts, feelings, and actions.

Chapter 57
Ready to Leap

When a life change is daunting but necessary

Periodically in life we are obliged to make a big change, whether or not we're really ready for it and whether or not we really want to make that change.

Maybe we need to leave a toxic marriage, a toxic job, a toxic country, or a toxic religion. People do not tend to make leaps of this sort either easily or quickly. They often hang around in a bad situation for years, all the while troubled and stewing.

Take marriage. Research and anecdotal evidence suggest that many people stay in toxic marriages for years—even for decades—after realizing they should leave. Some studies indicate that it can take an average of four to six years for someone to leave an unhealthy marriage. Of course, there are many factors at play: financial dependence, family pressures and the presence of children, hope that change may be possible, emotional manipulation, fear that the aftermath of divorce will prove worse than the marriage, legal barriers, low self-worth, and more.

Of course, there are reasons. But still: Four to six years after you know that the situation is toxic and that you should leave, and you are still there?

Or take work. In employment situations, the research indicates that folks stay in toxic jobs on average one to three years after realizing that they should leave. Many remain much longer, even for decades. Here, again, there are reasons, real and abundant reasons ranging from financial dependence to the fear of losing status and identity, from fear of change to misplaced loyalty. And who wants to search for a new job? Again, there are real factors involved in such delays.

Often there is a breaking point or a tipping point that decides the matter. All those reasons no longer count the way they did the moment before. A final insult tips the balance. One final indignity, and work becomes intolerable. This is the human way, to stick things out and to only make the leap—the leap you knew you were going to make—because of some painful happenstance.

Your brave new mind can help you do better.

As a philosophical matter, you announce the prime directive that you will leave toxic situations sooner rather than later. You add this as a key maxim to your life philosophy. When you're mistreated, you say to yourself, "No, I'm not going to ignore this. This thing that is happening matters." Maybe there will still be important reasons at play that prevent you from abandoning ship. But you stand ready to consider your options.

Because you are psychologically wise, you recognize that there may be emotional reasons for staying, and you talk yourself through each one of them. Fear of loss of identity? Your worry about what people will say? The fantasy that the situation might magically change? You think each of these through, giving each your full attention. You have zero doubt that many psychological hooks may be preventing you from escaping—and you bravely examine and unhook each one.

Because you are self-aware, you refuse to deny the reality of how bad the situation is. Having practiced getting under the radar of your own ego defenses, you know not to displace your upsetness onto your children, rationalize away blatant cruelty, repress your feelings and become ill, or in other ways hide the hard truth from yourself that the situation is really not okay. You are honest—and proud to be honest.

You do this by utilizing your well-stocked tool kit. You might use the tool of visualization by visualizing the change you would like to see. You might use the tool of journaling by writing in response to a prompt like, "What exactly am I afraid of that is keeping me from leaving?" You might use the tool of peer support and join a support group for people struggling to make this same transition, or by enlisting an ally who can help you create and execute an action plan. Wedged into a tight space of difficulty, you use your tools to help extricate yourself.

This talent of your brave new mind will save you years of pain and frustration. When a person knows that her marriage is absolutely over, research shows that she is likely to stay around another five years. Five years! Your brave new mind can help you get out in months. That's saving yourself years of despair.

Chapter 58
Ready for Red

On the benefits of splashes of color

Picture a gunmetal gray day. Nothing interesting has happened, or, you predict, can happen. The garbage disposal is cranky. Your remote job is both absurdly taxing and absurdly unimportant. And you have four more hours of work to go before you can stop and turn on the television.

You don't dare look at the world news—that is a terrible place to go. You don't dare do a diverting web search on the topic of the history of your small town, because that will lose you the afternoon. You only have your remote job to return to for hours, and dinner to think about, and that tragedy to deal with regarding your favorite show, which has new writers, and now, a terrible plot.

But what if you stood serenely ready for some small, bright splash of color to happen and to matter? In our Age of Collapse, that splash of color might amount to nothing more (and nothing less) than a brownie at the end of dinner, which on the one hand seems too trivial to count (and not even healthy, to boot), but on the other hand, is the kind of joy we can experience if we have made valuing small joys one of our prime directives.

There is a reason why a splash of red in an all-black painting affects us. It's just a bit of color against no color, after all, so why should it excite us, engage us, mesmerize us, or even matter? But it can, and it does. And whatever that phenomenon is, can't you have it in life? Can't there be little splashes of significance and joy no bigger than a brownie, or a memory, or a brief hug in the kitchen?

You could begin to better notice those splashes of red and even start exclaiming, "Oh, that was a nice splash!" This is an element of a certain philosophy of life: a philosophy of life that includes announcing that small things matter and that experiencing them matters as well. Might this become a part of your philosophy of life?

Think about it: If only big things are allowed to matter, how often will you experience life as mattering? Only when you win the Nobel Prize? Only when democracy returns? Only when you find your life partner? Yes, those are stellar, and more important than splashes of red, and things to be seriously hoped for. But in the meantime?

Is it possible for a person to say, "I am living for that bit of red"? Maybe. Isn't that how old folks in nursing homes live, organizing their days and their inner wellness around that dinner roll with butter or that afternoon television show? That dinner roll is almost enough to bring contentment and a reason to live another day, or maybe not even almost. One dinner roll. One splash of red. A good day.

"We are at ease with the idea that the beauty of a bird's song matters, even while people are still suffering in faraway places."

This may seem absurd, but we are easy with such absurdities. We are at ease with the idea that the beauty of a birdsong matters, even while people are still suffering in faraway places. We can usually accept having zero effect on the world, not today, when it is raining cats and dogs, and not tomorrow, when the rain continues. Isn't our species built this way, so that small joys matter, especially if we have chosen that as a prime directive?

And that splash of red might even prove momentous! A five-year-old child is watching a program and sees an amazing rock drummer perform. In a way that is both amazing and dreadful, somewhere deep inside of him a message is formed: "Rock drumming is great, and it's going to be my ticket out of this hick town!"

He is only five—but something just happened. I've had clients in the arts report exactly such occurrences. They were, as the Brits say, gobsmacked—utterly astonished by something they witnessed or experienced, and their whole life was suddenly given a direction, just like that.

It is a gray day. You are serenely ready for red; and blue; and violet; and maybe yellow, too. You aren't anxiously awaiting a color event. You are simply ready. It might be right around the corner, in the next room, between the umbrella stand and shoe rack. Maybe it will arrive in the form of a white rabbit. Who knows? Are you serenely ready for that?

Chapter 59
The Terrible Diagnosis

Serene readiness in the face of life's hardships

A splash of red is at one end of the spectrum, at the end where small joys reside. At the other end is terrible news. Is there a person alive who is ready for that?

No one is ready for, say, a cancer diagnosis—not serenely ready nor ready in any way. What you are is devastated; humiliated; deathly frightened—and not ready at all.

A client of mine was picnicking with her child. It was a lovely day by the river, and the child was playing on the bank. All was serene. The child cupped his hand and drank a little of the river water. Within days, he had died from cholera. There is nothing on earth that can lessen such a blow. It would have been no help to say, "It wasn't your fault" or "He's in a better place." There was nothing to say.

Maybe you need an operation and no doctor is available. Or maybe you're in a refugee camp that is being bombarded daily. Or maybe your adult child commits suicide. In any of these circumstances, you might be thinking, "Where does this guy get off telling me I should be serene?" Where do I get off guilt-tripping you about serenity in horrible situations and at such extreme moments? Isn't that both cruel and foolish of me?

Maybe it's possible that some Stoic philosopher, some cloistered monk, or some itinerant samurai might rise above terrible circumstances and face everything in life with perfect equanimity. But even if we grant that some few people are like that, sturdier and more philosophical than everyone else, the vast majority of us are not. If you cut us, we bleed. If you insult us, we hold a grudge. If we find ourselves in a horrible situation, we risk collapsing.

Still, maybe you can learn to be just a little bit readier? Maybe the four legs of our stool—a sturdy philosophy of life, psychological wisdom, self-awareness, and a full tool kit of tactics—can help support you at such terrible extremities. Maybe your brave new mind can make you a little readier to dispute self-accusations?

Of course, it certainly matters how awful the thing is. "We've caught it early" is a very different reality from "I'm terribly sorry, it's inoperable." But whatever the severity of the crisis, can you perhaps stand ready to befriend yourself? It is one thing to be devastated by a diagnosis. It is another thing, and an extra burden, to pile on and multiply the stress by being upset with yourself for feeling devastated.

You can be sad, frightened, overwhelmed, inconsolable. You can allow yourself to be human. There may not be any mind—whether a typical one or a brave new one—that is truly equal to disaster. But your brave new mind can at least help by supporting clarity, conviction, and resilience.

You stand ready to rebound. You might even whisper this private message to yourself: "I am going to feel what I need to feel, and then I am going to do the next right thing. My obligation to do the next right thing hasn't changed." Isn't that the essence of resilience? Won't you rebound more quickly if you are poised to do so? Isn't one of the readinesses we're after a readiness to spring back?

A person can promote resilience in all sorts of ways:

A sense of purpose
Optimism
Community support
Self-compassion
Strong relationships
Creating meaning from hardship
Humor as an intentional practice
Practicing gratitude

Any of these, or a combination of them, can help; and your brave new mind's serene readiness to bounce back can help. We are describing a way of life that is equal to life as it is actually experienced, even—or especially—on rainy days.

Chapter 60

Ready for Freedom

On the existential ideal of taking personal responsibility

What do I mean by a serene readiness to manifest our freedom and to take personal responsibility? Here's what it doesn't look like.

You face a challenge: say, whether or not to stay in touch with your aging, bullying parent. If you do not make a calm, intentional, thoughtful choice in this matter, it could mean on the one hand that you will continue to be bullied by your parent, or on the other hand that you will find yourself estranged from your parent without the matter ever having been aired between you, much less resolved.

In this scenario, you have not to date exercised your freedom to think clearly or to choose wisely. Now, however, your updated brave new mind allows for a better outcome. You serenely take full responsibility for acting consciously and thoughtfully. You are free to maintain a relationship with your parent, and you are equally free not maintain a relationship with your parent: What is required, though, are your careful deliberations.

Countless thinkers in the existential tradition have described the predicament we find ourselves in. The French philosopher Jean-Paul Sartre argued that we are "radically free," bereft of any predetermined essence, instructions, or path. We are fully obliged to create and sustain our own sense of meaning. In his estimation, most people flee from this realization and find themselves acting in *bad faith*, rationalizing and justifying their poor choices, and thereby making a mockery of the idea of free will.

The German philosopher Martin Heidegger declared that we should live with an acute *awareness of mortality* (*Sein-zum-Tode*, or '*being-toward-death*'), an awareness with the power to inspire us to live more meaningfully and not distract ourselves with inauthentic routines. A clear-eyed, truthful person, he argued, would recognize that life is finite and so would take conscious, deliberate steps to live authentically, rather than postponing fulfillment out of fear or social expectations.

The history of the idea of freedom in the face of the constraints of reality is a long and honored one. Our addition to this literature is the idea that all this can be serenely accepted as you go about the business of facing relentless, incontrovertible freedom. Freedom, along with its challenges, is now a given.

There is no longer any room for some vague hope that maybe life has a purpose, no more backsliding into philosophies of existence that make promises about an afterlife or a benevolent universe. We have turned that corner. And turning that corner typically comes with oodles of anxiety.

The Danish philosopher Søren Kierkegaard argued that freedom *must* come with anxiety. He held that this "dizziness," as he called it, naturally forced people to retreat into familiar roles in order to skip painful freedom. He explained, "He whose eye happens to look down into the yawning abyss becomes dizzy." Well, no longer.

Your brave new mind takes freedom as a given and sees it as no more worth getting anxious about than the worry that the universe will end in some billions of years. We are ready in many ways—and one way is our readiness to take our freedom as a given. Nothing to complain about; nothing to moan about; it just is.

We have turned that corner. Previously the specter of freedom came with all that anxiety. Now that anxiety has passed, just as a cyclone passes. We say, "This freedom may be unfortunate or exhilarating or whatever it may be, but it surely is, and I am calm about that."

Maybe you haven't turned that corner yet. But you can visualize where you would be if you did. If you did turn that corner, you would settle into the deepest understanding possible of what human freedom allows for and demands of you. And you would take in that knowledge not as a blow but with grace and ease. Can you see that?

Chapter 61

On Loyalty Oaths

When to take your own side and when to push back

Loyalty is another one of those tangled ideas. It is a word used by narcissists, fascists, authoritarians, and other bullies to stand for, "Never say a bad word against me, no matter how horrible I act." For a fascist leader, it is the demand that you stay silent and cower in fear. Otherwise you become an enemy. Those are the only two options: Either you are loyal, or you are an enemy.

Nationalistic loyalty, ethnic loyalty, religious loyalty, and even family loyalty all feel like traps, since the underlying command in each case is that you stick with your own side irrespective of who is right and who is wrong. Did your son murder someone? Help him escape. Is your country fighting an obscene war? Wave your flag. Is your town reinstituting segregation? Grin and bear it.

Loyalty.

At the same time, loyalty is a wonderful thing. Is there any better feeling than having someone loyally on our side? Does anything make us prouder than remaining loyal to a friend or loved one or taking the side of someone we respect? Internally, it means standing firmly on our own side and remaining loyal to our right to exist, loyal to our right to have opinions, and loyal to our right not to be abused—including by ourselves.

We are loyal to ourselves; at the same time, we stand ready to point out our own tricks, shadows, and shortfalls. Should we apologize to someone? Should we make amends? Then we do. Should we call ourselves on our lassitude, on our binges, on our chaotic thoughts? Then we do. We engage in hard truths and tough love. Like anyone who really wants the best for someone, we support ourselves while also firmly holding ourselves accountable.

What this means is that you stand ready to distinguish between loyalty of the first sort and loyalty of the second sort. You stay loyal to a friend through thick and thin; if she acts cruelly, however, you may not be able to be her friend any longer. You are ready for such moments to arrive, because they will. Likewise, you stand firmly on your own side, but you also face up, for instance, to the fact that you haven't paid any real attention to your life purposes in a month. You are ready for such reckonings.

Loyalty oaths of the bad kind have a long history, one that goes all the way back to the dawn of our species. In ancient Rome, soldiers and public officials swore loyalty oaths to the state or the emperor. During the Middle Ages, feudal vassals swore oaths of loyalty to their lords in exchange for land and protection. In England, the 1534 Oath of Supremacy required subjects to acknowledge the king as the supreme head of the Church of England. Refusal was not a good idea.

In the United States, we have seen our share, too, from Civil War loyalty oaths (both sides demanded them), to World War I loyalty oaths where you swore that you were not pro-German, to the Cold War and McCarthyism. We know why these loyalty oaths appear and reappear. Undemocratic leaders want uncritical allegiance.

With regard to ourselves, we are after self-love, not a servile, fearful, coerced loyalty. True loyalty to the self means not accepting everything the self proposes and not being afraid to resist the self's shadier propositions. We take a fundamental position of positive self-regard, but we are also truthful.

Our brave new mind stands ready to loyally support us and loyally call us out. Support is its first objective. We are first of all obliged to affirm ourselves. We can't do without that one best friend, ourselves. And like a good friend, we share hard truths with ourselves. Our brave new mind is serenely ready for that, too.

Chapter 62
Ready for surprises
Including the surprise that is us

Where did that thought come from? Where did that behavior come from? Remember our dynamic succession of thoughts and feelings? Well, what's coming around the corner next? Is it a thought about lunch? A self-recrimination? A bright idea for a novel that commits us for the next two years to the hard labor of bringing it to fruition? Or a flash of anger?

With regard to our thoughts and behaviors, we can guess at what's coming next, but we can't predict it. Still, we can get ready! That's so very important. We can't make predictions, but we can stand ready.

Let's drill down on this idea of readiness from the point of view of chaos theory and complexity theory, two bodies of thought that attempt to describe how complex systems (like the brain) function.

Consider. You get an email pitching an informational webinar coming up in just a few minutes where you'll learn all about a new retreat center in Costa Rica. Two things might then happen: You might ignore that email; or it might catch your eye, you might go on that call, and a year from now, you might find yourself leading a workshop in Costa Rica.

Can you predict which reaction you'll have? No. But you can take a split second and make a quick, informed decision, deciding, for instance, to skip that informational call on the grounds that your life purposes will not be served by you distracting yourself with thoughts about workshops in Costa Rica.

Chaos theory is a branch of mathematics that studies complex systems whose behavior is highly sensitive to initial conditions and to subsequent conditions. This sensitivity is colloquially called "the butterfly effect": the idea that a butterfly flapping its wings in the Amazon jungle might through a long series of events and happenstances affect the weather in Omaha.

Well, consider all the flapping that goes on in your mind. We've likened that to a dynamic succession of thoughts and feelings, but it is wildly more chaotic, interactive, and disorderly than that. It is rather more like particles colliding in a super-collider. Who knows what particle will flare up or die out? No one. Yes, there are rules and principles to discern and predictions to make. But in the context of sheer chaos!

Chaos theory suggests that personality is not static or linear. Small changes in a person's environment and experiences can lead to significant, unpredictable changes in behavior or personality traits. For example, minor life events or stressors may lead to profound shifts in emotional or behavioral responses. You miss the bus, and something snaps in you and you take yourself off on a vision quest. You get a rejection letter from just the first of the dozen colleges where you applied, and you decide not to go to college. And so on.

The grave impacts of these chaotic reactions explain why it is desperately important that we stand ready to deal with this human reality of unpredictability. If we are ready, then there is just enough space between the bus pulling away and our decision to go on a vision quest to challenge that hasty decision. If we are ready, there is just enough space between opening that rejection letter and deciding not to go to college to dispute that dramatic disavowal. That space may only be a second or a microsecond. But if we are ready, that is all that we need.

You can sense a prime directive here. Let me say it, first in many words and then in just a few words. The long version: "Because I am not really in charge of what thought will pop up next since that thought is the product of real complexity and chaos, it should not surprise me that the next thought I think might not serve me, might not be welcome, might prove a distraction, might be false, and so on. Rather than reacting with surprise and chiding myself for thinking something I would prefer not to think, and rather than mindlessly allowing that thought to fill my mind, I will spend a split second deciding how I want to react to that thought."

The short version: "My thoughts require inspection. I am ready for that. My actions do too. I stand ready to bring awareness to both."

Neither the idea of "free will" nor the idea of "determinism" quite captures what is going on in the mind. In one sense, everything is determined. But that doesn't make your next thought or your next action predictable. There will be reasons why you refuse to write your novel or why you decide to write your novel. But the collisions going on inside your brain make predicting which way you will go impossible. We may have a hunch—but a surprise may be coming!

Our brave new mind stands unsurprised. Yes, maybe we didn't expect that odd thought. Maybe we didn't expect that we are thinking about doing something "completely out of character." All right; so be it. We have the power to think rather than to stand surprised or to react blindly. That is what our brave new mind can do.

Chapter 63

Some Other You Is Lurking

Serenely ready for surprising identity shifts

You are certain that you are you. You know your preferences; you know your reactions; you know your personality. You see yourself as rational, steady, and relatively unflappable. Then something happens: It doesn't seem like much—and yet you discover that your identity is threatened. You were you, and now you are some other you. Are you ready for that possibility?

Picture something as simple and straightforward as the power going out. You can't watch television. You can't turn on a light. Your refrigerator stops working. Your connection to the world feels like it's ending, once the batteries on your phone and computer die. Are you the "same person" when such an event happens?

Imagine the power staying out for days. Are you still you?

What if it lasted for months? Who would you become? A more frightened person? A more ruthless person? Someone huddled in a corner? Someone out at night, looking to steal power? Someone hallucinating ghosts? Someone edgier, someone angrier, someone paralyzed?

What if it lasted forever? What if there was no more electricity? Would you still be you or some unrecognizable you?

And is there a sense of how you can stand serenely ready today for the possibility of such identity dissolutions tomorrow?

There is a reality television show where survivalists are dropped into the wilderness and must outlast the other competitors in order to win a very substantial prize. They all think they can do it—they are all survivalists, after all. But within not too many days, a substantial number of the contestants start to break down. They looked to be "psychologically strong" when they arrived. Now, they look to be significantly weakened versions of themselves, really barely a shell of themselves. In just days!

Some ask to leave after just a few hours.

When they give up and return home, do they become themselves again? Or are they now a changed version of themselves? By virtue of that televised failure, are they a shadow of themselves? Less confident? More anxious? More irritable? Or even completely ruined?

And why were they so unready for the experience they knew was coming? They knew they would be alone! Why did that wilderness experience take them so much by surprise?

Let us chalk this up as one of the mysteries of human nature. But we do have an important takeaway. We are obliged to keep an awareness tucked away in a corner of consciousness that for whatever reason—a change in circumstance, some strange, unaccountable inner shift, a realization, a stray, overheard remark, a who-knows-what—our current identity may dissolve and some new self, whether we like it or not, may suddenly appear.

Maybe it's a big event that happens. What might homelessness do to a person? Prolonged unemployment? The death of a spouse? Or maybe it's something objectively small: overhearing a friend calling you fat, overhearing the director remark that you were hired as a favor and how he wished that you had a shred of talent. Maybe it is nothing more than a passing thought in that dynamic succession of thoughts and feelings, the passing thought that you've become old and invisible. And, just like that, a new, maybe weaker, maybe sadder identity is hatched. Just like that.

We do not want to dwell on this possibility, but we do want to stand serenely ready to catch ourselves in such moments. You overhear that terrible remark: You want your next thought to be "Don't change your self-image!" rather than "I'm fat and hopeless!" or "I'm a no-talent fraud!" Because you were serenely ready for exactly such an occurrence, you spare your identity a real knock on the head.

Identity can be disturbed. It can even dissolve into a puddle. As with a terrible medical diagnosis or an armed invasion, we can't really "get ready" for such strange, unsettling, even catastrophic events. But our brave new mind can certainly hold the idea that identity is a fragile possession and needs our attention and our protection.

If you want to remain you, you need to stay alert. Some other you may be lurking right around the corner, ready to present you with some unwanted version of yourself.

Chapter 64

Acquiring Serene Readiness

Whether in an instant or over the
long haul

I have no roadmap to get you to your brave new mind. In a
certain sense, you can just teleport yourself there by flipping a
switch and deciding to be both more serene and readier.
People do sometimes change from one minute to the next.
Sometimes it is in the downward direction of giving up.
Sometimes it is in the direction of affirmation and effort.
Maybe you can just blink and instantly arrive at your desired
destination?

Change of this sort can indeed happen in the blink of an eye.
The brain's billions of neurons, operating across a universe of
chaos and complexity, come to a simple, certain conclusion:
this. In our case, it opts for the following: "I am going all in on
serene readiness." Well, that is possible; and if that happens,
if you just teleport yourself there, that would be great.

But probably for the vast majority of folks, yourself included, it
will prove more of a journey than a miracle. What can help on
that journey? All of the following.

1. You set the clear intention to become serenely ready. You clarify the concept in your own mind and remind yourself why the idea matters.

2. You visualize yourself as serenely ready. You picture yourself reacting with serene readiness in a variety of situations: when you're surprised by an impulse, when you're reluctant to take care of business, etc.

3. You affirm your intentions and repeat encouraging statements to yourself, statements like "I am doing the next right thing" and "I am ready for this." You announce that you can grow, heal, change, and arrive at your destination.

4. You break down the big goal of achieving serene readiness into smaller, doable steps. For instance, you create one "serene readiness" ceremony that helps you overcome your natural resistance to public performance.

5. You frankly and forthrightly address your fears. Afraid to resist your dictator's latest draconian measures? Terrified of reprisals if you dare speak? Air that fear, with an eye to seeing if resistance is possible.

6. Practice breathing techniques or other anxiety management techniques that help reduce any natural anxiety that may be getting in the way of the practice of serene readiness.

7. Create a "support team" (which might be just one friend) and share your goals and intentions. Maybe the two of you can work on serene readiness together.

8. You might journal your hesitations, examine in writing what's blocking you, and explore your options and potential solutions.

9. You might create checklists, maybe one for each area where you are hoping to grow more serenely ready, and use your checklists to prioritize tasks and stay organized. Likewise, you might create schedules and block in time for your multiple life purposes.

10. You might start a success journal and keep track of your wins. Did you surprise yourself by reacting with serene readiness to a sudden conflict that would have previously sent you into a tailspin? Notice and record that victory.

11. Prepare so as to be ready. Are you ready to write your novel if you can't find your files or your notes? Are you ready to lose twenty pounds if your freezer is full of ice cream? Get your environment ready.

12. Engage in general self-care. This would include taking care that you get enough sleep, disengage from toxic relationships, eat well, exercise, hydrate, declutter, eliminate stressors from your life, and so on. Create your self-care agenda and follow it.

13. Work on your philosophy of life and your prime directives. Settle into your self-directed, self-organized picture of life. What matters? How will you comport yourself? Get a good picture of life as you intend to live it.

14. Work on psychological wisdom. Spend time deciphering how your mind works and how the minds of others work. What saddens you? How can you make some meaning? How can you resolve any long-simmering conflicts? This is important knowledge!

15. You might start very small and take just the tiniest first step so as to get started and begin to build some momentum.

Changing in an instant is rather magical. Practicing the above good habits is nothing like magic. It is just work—righteous work, but still just work. It may prove a journey of a thousand miles, with a heavy backpack on. It would be marvelous if it happened all in an instant. But if it's the long journey instead, so be it.

Chapter 65
Safely Not Paying Attention

Conscious and not conscious, alert and dreamy

The following is hard to put into words because it will sound contradictory. On the one hand, you want to be alert and ready. On the other hand, there are plenty of times when you want to dream, rather than deal with reality. If you are working out your understanding of the nature of the chemical bond, you do not want to know the day's stock prices, contemplate a stray thought about the in-laws visiting, or allow a self-recrimination to settle—or even be heard.

This is confusing because you may need to both work out your understanding of the nature of the chemical bond, employing some billions of neurons on that task, while also allowing some billions of neurons to "silently" figure out where the in-laws are going to sleep. The brain can and does do this. But it's complicated, isn't it?

If we wanted to create a sentence that does this dilemma justice, it would be: "Please, brain, pay full attention to the chemical bond thing, and if you want to do a little thinking about the in-laws at the same time, go right ahead, but please don't bother me about it unless you come up with a solution, which you can certainly tell me about, unless I am right on the brink of solving my puzzle, in which case, file it away and tell me later."

This is a completely sensible request to make of one's mind. But in real life, people often do not feel safe enough to give their genuinely full attention to a train of thought. My creative clients and the coaches I train have a lot of trouble feeling safe not noticing this or that stray worry. The stray worry might be, "Is this sentence really grammatically correct?" or "Should I add 10% to the prices of my paintings to cover inflation?" or "Can I call myself a coach if I'm not certified?"

What feels so unsafe about possibly putting a sentence into the world without a proper comma? Objectively, this is beyond trivial. What must be going on underneath is the following conversation, happening in quick time: "If I put out that incorrect sentence, someone somewhere will call me on it, and that will make me feel terrible, and it might even ruin me." And that last part sticks: the thought that an incorrect sentence is the road to ruination.

This writer has gone from what is not even a remote possibility—the idea that a sentence with a flaw can ruin him— to something like a certainly that he will be ruined if he lets that sentence out. Why are we built that way, so that we can go from less than a remote possibility to the absolute certainty of an impending catastrophe in a nanosecond, and for no good reason? Shouldn't there be a pill that cures this (and remove wrinkles at the same time)?

We want to be spared this. We want a quiet mind. There are times when we want to know nothing, or next to nothing, about our dynamic succession of thoughts and feelings; nothing, or next to nothing, about what's going in the next room; nothing, or next to nothing, about what's going on in the world. We want zero interruptions if we are trying to dream up the ending to our short story or the bridge to our song. Isn't that exactly how that blessed creative flow state feels, as if we've silenced everything for the sake of following a train of thought?

I would like to present you with this offering, neatly gift wrapped: You can achieve that silence and then feel safe in it. You will still be ready, serenely ready. Your mind will still be poised to notice what it needs to notice. There is a world of difference between being calmly present for action and being nervously worried about everything going on around you and inside of you. Vigilance is a feature of our early warning system alerting us to danger, and it has its place. But it must not have carte blanche!

It is safe to temporarily ignore this for the sake of paying attention to that. You are still serenely ready, for a turn of events, for a revelation that must break through, for the door bell ringing. Remember: If you can't safely decide not to pay attention to all that noisy chatter and all those prospective doubts and worries, you won't be able to think.

Chapter 66

The Siren's Call to Oblivion

Standing ready to refute meaninglessness

Sometimes we just don't want to bother.

Please, life, just leave me alone. Please, life, go away. Who needs another day of this? Who needs another insult, another indignity, another injustice? Who needs all this pain? Who needs all this meaninglessness? Who needs another diet, another hour at the gym, more physical therapy? Who needs another philosophy, more of somebody else's pointless opinions? Who needs the sun, the bustle, the whole new-day thing?

Give me oblivion.

Organizing your life around your life purposes is a good idea. That is a cornerstone of a philosophy of life that is likely to work for you. But doing this presupposes that things matter to you. It won't work to say this is important to me and that is important to me if nothing is actually important to you. If nothing matters to you, including whether or not you live, that opens the window wide to the siren's call to oblivion. Do you hear it?

It is a very attractive and very soothing call. But is embracing it your next right thing?

Instead, we stand ready for meaninglessness. It hardly surprises us; it hardly daunts us. We face it by saying the following:

"Okay, nothing feels particularly meaningful to me at the moment. Nothing feels important. In fact, very little has ever felt important to me. Meaning has always been a problem. But I am deeply aware that meaning comes and goes and is just off on vacation right now. Maybe it has been on vacation my whole life. But I expect it back. And I will welcome it.

"In the meantime, I am going to artificially assert that the following things are important to me and that these are reasons enough not to opt for oblivion. I know this artificial asserting is rather absurd and something of a game, but it is the right game to play. It keeps me in the game of life. And you know, I think I can maybe hear meaning flapping its wings and returning from its trip..."

Your brave new mind stands serenely ready to assert importance. This sounds like, "It is important that I get up." This sounds like, "It is important that I hug the ones I love." This sounds like, "It is important that I respect my own efforts." This sounds like, "Given humanity's pain, it's important that I be of a little service." This is job number one of our brave new mind, to assert importance even if we are not feeling that importance.

If a thing feels intrinsically important, wonderful. But if nothing feels intrinsically important, you announce that is unacceptable. You do not accept that the absence of importance can't be disputed. You dispute this insignificance energetically. You shout from the rooftops, "I deem this important, and that! That is the gauntlet I throw down to life!"

Oblivion is a sad, sweet song. It feels like just closing your eyes and floating away. There, right over there, just beyond the stratosphere, is the gentle embrace of the universe; what a tempting call. In Huxley's *Brave New World*, soma, the state-sanctioned drug, provides an easy escape from pain, discomfort, and serious thought, allowing citizens to sink into a blissful, consequence-free oblivion. So as to deepen that oblivion, the World State erases personal identity and strong emotions, ensuring that people remain complacent and never experience true suffering. Here is a passage that offers insight:

> *By this time, the soma had begun to work. Eyes shone, cheeks were flushed, the inner light of universal benevolence broke out on every face in happy, friendly smiles. Even Bernard felt himself a little melted. He too was smiling. When the Director made his great speech, Bernard managed to beam. 'Absolute bliss,' he said to himself as he made his way back to the temporary haven of his rooms. "Absolute oblivion."*

Well, we do not accept this sad, happy state. We stand ready to reply to that siren call with a shout of defiance. Meaninglessness, you say? No, thank you!

Chapter 67

The Ambition to Be Human

Whether calm seas or heavy weather
are on the horizon

I'm guessing that you have the following four ambitions.

You have the ambition to understand what it means to be human; that is, you have a thirst for understanding. You have the ambition to accept what it means to be human; that is, you have a thirst for self-acceptance. You have the ambition to play out your human potential; that is, you have a thirst for manifestation. And you have the ambition to be a responsible human being; that is, you have a thirst for moral action.

Isn't this you?

Our brave new mind serves these ambitions. The better we master serene readiness, the better we come to recognize what is going on behind the scenes in our mind, and the better we understand that our readiness is less about waiting and more about orienting and choosing. We choose to understand. We are ready for that. We choose to accept. We are ready for that. We choose to manifest. We are ready for that. We choose to be righteous. We are ready for that.

Employing our existential intelligence, our executive function, our whole brain, or whatever we opt to call it, we orient our mind in the direction of personal choosing. We say without needing to say the words: "Yes, all this churning is definitely going on inside of me and outside of me. But I stand ready to live my life purposes on the one hand, and to deal with what life throws at me on the other."

This is what "readiness" means. It doesn't mean just waiting for something to happen and then reacting to it. It isn't just anticipation. It isn't just the coil of a spring or potential energy. It is a stream of doing, punctuated by course corrections when something must be handled.

Picture a sailor in a sailboat. She is sailing. She is doing the things she needs to do from moment to moment to keep on course. She is serenely living, doing one right next thing after another. But she is also noticing: She is noticing the look of the sky, which alerts her that weather is coming. She gets ready for that, as ready as she can. She surrenders to the fact that she can't prevent a storm from coming, while at the same time readying herself for that storm.

Maybe she changes direction to try to avoid the storm or to try to get back to shore. She is decisive; she chooses. She is practiced at sailing, and so she has prepared herself all along for just such situations. She turns her small sailboat around and heads for shore. She isn't upset, disappointed, or regretful. She simply relaxes into the moment and returns to shore.

Or maybe the weather evaporates and the sea calms. Then she may sit back for a moment, smile, thank Poseidon for this momentary respite, and return to her original course. But she knows that the seas will roil again and that storms will surely come. She hasn't suddenly lost her understanding of her predicament as a lone sailor in a churning ocean. Nor is she surprised when the next storm appears on the horizon. She is ready and is serene in the knowledge that this is what is.

We have all sorts of ambitions. A writer might have the ambition to write an outstanding novel and have it become a bestseller. A software engineer might have the ambition to get in on the ground floor of a mega-successful start-up. A sailor might have the ambition to own her own boat and sail the seven seas. And you and I have the ambition to be human. That is exactly the right kind of ambition.

Chapter 68

A Certain Hope

What to keep, what to jettison?

One central reason that you might opt to do the work required of you to acquire this brave new mind could be because you haven't given up on hope. Yes, hope has been fading. But as the old saw has it, hope also springs eternal.

But what sort of hope is the right hope for today? Some outdated hope for miracles, progress, humanity, and fairness? Or a new hope rooted in the availability of an authentic response to what life throws at us? How should we conceptualize "modern hope"?

"Hope" can confuse us. Most traditions both invite you not to hope—to leave matters to gods, to detach, to accept, to not worry your head about outcomes—while at the same time painting pictures that are meant to feel hopeful: pictures of heavens, nirvana, never having to return again to face the suffering of existence, and so on. Yes, it's true your prayers may not be answered—please don't hope for that—but a gigantic prize is waiting for you just over the horizon, these pictures seem to say. This parlor trick confuses.

On balance, many traditions advise us not to hope and urge us not to put our eggs in that basket. Zen Buddhism asks us to strive for nonattachment, equanimity, and a rather stark embrace of the present moment. Taoism advocates for *wu wei*, or effortless action, the idea of acting in harmony with the natural flow of life without striving for specific outcomes. Stoicism teaches that we should accept what's beyond our control, focus on cultivating virtue, and not hope for a better or different future. In short, no hope, please.

While Christianity emphasizes placing hope in God's promises, especially of eternal life, Christian mystics and contemplatives have focused on surrendering to God's will and trusting in divine providence without clinging to any specific hopes. No hope, please.

Hindu philosophy, particularly in texts like the *Bhagavad Gita*, teaches the importance of performing one's duty (or *dharma*) without attachment to the fruits of actions. Another version of no hope, please.

The Sufi mystic thread in Islam focuses on union with the Divine, which involves letting go of personal desires and hopes and trusting in God's will. Like the others, this is a version of no hope, please.

Various modern traditions, from secular humanism to existentialism to twelve-step programs, provide their contemporary spins on the idea of nonattachment. Existentialist philosophers like Jean-Paul Sartre and Albert Camus address the idea of living without inherent hope or meaning. We are to create personal meaning and purpose in a seemingly indifferent universe and then live fully (if absurdly) without hope.

We come up against what looks like a paradox. We are to live fully and authentically without hope, existentialists say. But one primary goal of existential psychotherapy and existential coaching is renewed hope. This paradox unravels when we come to understand that "hope" does not mean false reassurance or superficial optimism. Rather, it is the sense of authentic, engaged, meaningful existence that we have been discussing throughout this book.

This "new hope" is the serene readiness to live in the exact world that we experience, facing death, freedom, anxiety, isolation, and all the rest as serenely and as instrumentally as we can manage.

The desirability of this new hope—or of any hope—can't be based on examples. We could trade examples endlessly. You could tell me a hideous story of human trafficking, and I might reply with a story of remarkable service. You might point to a kindness, and I might point out a terror. We could trade such examples forever since both sorts of examples exist in abundance. Neither set of examples can help us determine where we want to come down on the question of hope or hopelessness.

The answer isn't a calculation: It is a decision. I hope that you will decide to hope—in the contemporary sense of the word, betting on your ability to navigate the project of your life with grace and self-respect. That might mean in one situation hanging on or attaching and in another situation letting go. You stand serenely ready for either response to life. That is my hope for you.

Chapter 69
Prime Directives Revisited

Your ten commandments, give
or take

I think you now have a pretty good picture of what serene readiness means and what it might look like in your life.

To achieve such a useful, ambitious state might take a lifetime of work; and that is fine, as what other work is more important?

But it would be even better if it could be acquired sooner rather than later—even in the blink of an eye, as we discussed earlier. What might help it arrive that quickly and help it remain in place are some number of prime directives that amount to a shorthand approximation of your philosophy of life.

We looked at how the slogans of the 12-step world, slogans like "First things first" and "Easy does it," help tremendously in keeping individuals in recovery alert, comforted, and on track. They are a recovering alcoholic's or addict's prime directives.

Let me share with you a few of my own prime directives, some of which I've mentioned already.

One is "Do the next right thing." For me, this stands for a lot. It is a combination of "do the next ethical thing" and "do the next appropriate thing" with "stay ready" and "be active." It carries many messages in a neat five words.

Another is just the single word "Process." "Process" stands for "Show up without attaching to outcomes," "Accept that not everything you do will be brilliant," "Remember that the work comes with no guarantees," "Be easy with the truth that everyone has an opinion," and more.

A third is "Sooner rather than later." This one is rather self-explanatory. It stands for "Stay out of your own way," "Say less rather than more," "Respond quickly," and "Keep moving forward."

A fourth is "Stay skeptical." This is a lifelong stance of mine that is even more important to me now than ever before. I have written whole books skeptical of religion, psychiatry, and other sacred cows, and I respect—maybe even revere—the archetype of the whistleblower.

A fifth is "Do not need this to be easy." This alerts me to complain less than I otherwise might when a book I'm writing is not working, when a book is going out of print, when a book is selling only a handful of copies, and so on. A variation is "No expectations of ease, please."

A sixth is "No rabbit holes." Like everyone, I am tempted to engage in "Internet research" that is really just a contemporary way of avoiding doing the next right thing.

There are more rabbit holes today than ever before, almost more rabbit holes than solid ground. So this one is good to remember!

A seventh is "People are people." This one helps me to stand unsurprised by what people do. Did someone not follow through on a promise? I am not outraged. Is someone much less nice than he appears in public? I am not shocked. "People are people."

An eighth is "Be of some help." This one reminds me that my goals are modest and humane: No big words like "transformation" or "salvation," just a helping hand.

If you stop and create your own set of prime directives, will you then always do the next right thing or never go down some rabbit hole? Of course not. But those prime directives will help. They will help you live the life you want to live, one that makes you proud.

The alternative is to live without prime directives and the philosophy of life they encapsulate and support. That typically amounts to a life of chaos, doubt, uncertainty, and a center that doesn't hold. Without prime directives, we tend to act rather randomly and incline toward our default meaning substitutes—toward the Scotch, the shopping spree, the hours of indolence.

If this were a self-help workbook, I would next invite you to engage in some exercises. "Make a list of your prime directives, order them and prioritize them," and so on. This isn't that book. Let me just invite you to meditate on the value of prime directives and their relationship to the goal of serene readiness. Aren't you both more serene and readier for life if you know, for instance, that what's next is "the next right thing"? Consider.

Chapter 70
Picture Yourself
Some last words on serene readiness

Let me refresh your memory as to the purpose of this book.

Minds are crashing. Millions upon millions of people are on the verge of psychological collapse and catastrophe. These collapses, crashes, and catastrophes are being called by all sorts of names, usually as part of the phrase "an epidemic of": an epidemic of depression; an epidemic of anxiety; an epidemic of job dissatisfaction; an epidemic of hopelessness; an epidemic of addiction; and so on.

All roads lead to the same place. The world has changed. It is not the world of our grandfathers and grandmothers. It is not the world of our fathers and mothers. We could create a very long laundry list of these changes: nuclear weapons, artificial intelligence, late-stage capitalism, globalism, social media, the new oligarchs, revitalized fascism, endless screen time, the commercialization and medicalization of everything, and so on. It is a very long, dreary, overwhelming list.

The only aspect of this contemporary situation that we can control is our own mind. And we need a new one of those to meet these challenging times. I am calling that our "brave new mind" and asserting that its central feature is the serene readiness to deal with the reality of our current circumstances.

I hope that I've painted a clear and useful picture of both aspects of that serene readiness, the "serene" part and the "readiness" part. I hope that you can picture yourself serenely ready, see the value in achieving that state, and will work toward achieving it. It can support you and save you like nothing else can.

Remember the four legs of that sturdy stool I described to you. You have a philosophy of life that supports both serenity and action. You are psychologically acute. You are in excellent self-relationship. And you possess all sorts of inner tools that support both serenity and readiness. There you are, complete, wise, human, ready. That is a place to aspire to.

Maybe something dire or dramatic happens. You are still ready, as ready as a human being can be. That is all you can ask of yourself, to be as ready as possible. And maybe nothing is happening. Then you simply live your life purposes. You can always be serenely ready for that. You can always stand ready to do the next right thing, to follow your own prime directives, to choose, amend, and live your life purposes.

Maybe you hug a loved one because she is nearby. Maybe you open your laptop and donate to a cause. Maybe you work on your symphony. Maybe you send out seven emails in support of your business. Maybe you exercise. Perhaps you have your menu of life purposes posted on the refrigerator (and in your mind), and rather than grab a snack out of the refrigerator, you grab a purpose.

I don't have an answer about how you can change the world. But I do have an answer as to how you can respond to the world. You can respond with serene readiness. That is your best bet. You stand serenely ready to create, to relate, to love, to act, to do good. You opt to honor the freedom you possess. Isn't that your ideal?

And maybe you will teach this to your children, too. They are bound to find themselves quite at sea in this brave new world of ours. They may grow dark and frightened as they look out around them. They may lose hope, just as you and I may lose hope. You can help them get ready—serenely ready. Shouldn't that be one of your life purposes and prime directives?

Your mind is the work. How you design it, how you instruct it, how you manage it determines how you will feel and how you will act. Invite it to stand serenely ready for what is coming. Becoming ready for joy, ready for action, ready for surprises—serenely ready for everything—is a vision to embrace and a practice to build.

About Eric Maisel

Eric Maisel, PhD (Counseling Psychology), has written more than 60 books and has edited an additional dozen. After majoring in psychology and philosophy, he went on to earn graduate degrees in creative writing, counseling, and counseling psychology. A retired licensed MFT, he is an active diplomat coach (the highest international coaching designation), and his *Psychology Today* blog "Rethinking Mental Health" has more than three million views.

He is the lead editor for the Critical Psychology and Critical Psychiatry series published by the Ethics International Press, and in conjunction with Noble-Manhattan Coaching, he has developed three worldwide training programs, a Creativity Coach Certificate Program, an Existential Wellness Coach Certificate Program, and a Relationship Coach Certificate Program.

Dr. Maisel has been interviewed more than 500 times and has presented scores of keynotes, workshops, and lectures worldwide to organizations including the International Society for Ethical Psychology and Psychiatry, the American Mental

Health Counselors Association, the Savannah College of Art and Design, the American Conservatory Theater, and the International Conference for Existential Psychotherapy. He maintains an international coaching practice.

Please visit Dr. Maisel at https://www.ericmaisel.com or contact him at: ericmaisel@hotmail.com

Books That Save Lives came into being in 2024 when the editor and publisher, Brenda Knight, heard directly from readers and authors that certain self-help, grief, psychology books, and journals were providing a lifeline for folks. We live in a stressful world where it is increasingly difficult not to feel overwhelmed, worried, depressed, and downright scared. We intend to offer support for the vulnerable, including people struggling with mental wellness and physical illness as well as people of color, queer and trans adults and teens, immigrants and anyone who needs encouragement and inspiration.

From first responders, military veterans, and retirees to LGBTQ+ teens and to those experiencing the shock of bereavement and loss, our books have saved lives. To us, there is no higher calling.

We would love to hear from you! Our readers are our most important resource; we value your input, suggestions, and ideas.

Please stay in touch with us and follow us at:

www.booksthatsavelives.net

Instagram: @booksthatsavelives

www.ingramcontent.com/pod-product-compliance
Lightning Source LLC
Chambersburg PA
CBHW020243290326
41930CB00038B/230